PENTESTING 101

CRACKING GADGETS AND HACKING SOFTWARE

4 BOOKS IN 1

BOOK 1
PENTESTING 101: A BEGINNER'S GUIDE TO ETHICAL HACKING

BOOK 2
PENTESTING 101: EXPLOITING VULNERABILITIES IN NETWORK SECURITY

BOOK 3
PENTESTING 101: ADVANCED TECHNIQUES FOR WEB APPLICATION SECURITY

BOOK 4
PENTESTING 101: MASTERING CYBERSECURITY CHALLENGES AND BEYOND

ROB BOTWRIGHT

Published by Rob Botwright
Library of Congress Cataloging-in-Publication Data
ISBN 978-1-83938-638-1
Cover design by Rizzo

Disclaimer

The contents of this book are based on extensive research and the best available historical sources. However, the author and publisher make no claims, promises, or guarantees about the accuracy, completeness, or adequacy of the information contained herein. The information in this book is provided on an "as is" basis, and the author and publisher disclaim any and all liability for any errors, omissions, or inaccuracies in the information or for any actions taken in reliance on such information. The opinions and views expressed in this book are those of the author and do not necessarily reflect the official policy or position of any organization or individual mentioned in this book. Any reference to specific people, places, or events is intended only to provide historical context and is not intended to defame or malign any group, individual, or entity. The information in this book is intended for educational and entertainment purposes only. It is not intended to be a substitute for professional advice or judgment. Readers are encouraged to conduct their own research and to seek professional advice where appropriate. Every effort has been made to obtain necessary permissions and acknowledgments for all images and other copyrighted material used in this book. Any errors or omissions in this regard are unintentional, and the author and publisher will correct them in future editions.

BOOK 1 - PENTESTING 101: A BEGINNER'S GUIDE TO ETHICAL HACKING

BOOK 2 - PENTESTING 101: EXPLOITING VULNERABILITIES IN NETWORK SECURITY

BOOK 3 - PENTESTING 101: ADVANCED TECHNIQUES FOR WEB APPLICATION SECURITY

BOOK 4 - PENTESTING 101: MASTERING CYBERSECURITY CHALLENGES AND BEYOND

Introduction

In an age where our lives are intricately connected to the digital realm, the need for cybersecurity has never been more critical. The constant evolution of technology brings both innovation and new vulnerabilities, making it imperative to stay one step ahead of potential threats. Welcome to the world of ethical hacking and cybersecurity, where understanding the minds of hackers and securing our digital landscapes are paramount.

This book bundle, "PENTESTING 101: CRACKING GADGETS AND HACKING SOFTWARE," comprises four volumes that will take you on a journey through the fascinating, challenging, and ever-evolving field of ethical hacking. Whether you are a beginner looking to explore the fundamentals or an experienced cybersecurity professional seeking to sharpen your skills, these books offer a comprehensive guide to ethical hacking, network security, web application security, and advanced cybersecurity techniques.

BOOK 1 - PENTESTING 101: A BEGINNER'S GUIDE TO ETHICAL HACKING In this introductory volume, we lay the groundwork for your ethical hacking journey. You will learn how to set up your hacking environment, understand the hacker mindset, and employ scanning and enumeration techniques to uncover vulnerabilities. By the end of this book, you will have a solid foundation in ethical hacking and be ready to explore more advanced topics.

BOOK 2 - PENTESTING 101: EXPLOITING VULNERABILITIES IN NETWORK SECURITY Diving deeper into the realm of network security, this volume equips you with the knowledge and tools to exploit vulnerabilities in network protocols, gain unauthorized access to network resources, and safely intercept network traffic. Network security is at the heart of modern cybersecurity, and this book will empower you to defend and secure networks effectively.

BOOK 3 - PENTESTING 101: ADVANCED TECHNIQUES FOR WEB APPLICATION SECURITY The third installment focuses on web application security, a domain where vulnerabilities can have far-reaching consequences. You will explore the landscape of web application security, delve into authentication and session management testing, and uncover advanced vulnerabilities. With this knowledge, you will be prepared to safeguard web applications against the ever-present threat of cyberattacks.

BOOK 4 - PENTESTING 101: MASTERING CYBERSECURITY CHALLENGES AND BEYOND The final book in this bundle takes your skills to the pinnacle of ethical hacking. It introduces advanced network penetration testing techniques, explores the world of IoT and embedded systems exploitation, and addresses challenges in cloud security. Additionally, you will learn to apply your expertise in real-world ethical hacking scenarios, manage incidents, conduct digital forensics, and advance your career in the field.

Whether you are motivated by the desire to protect your organization, bolster your cybersecurity career, or simply satiate your curiosity about the world of ethical hacking, "PENTESTING 101: CRACKING GADGETS AND HACKING SOFTWARE" has something to offer. Throughout this journey, we emphasize ethical hacking as a force for good, aimed at identifying vulnerabilities and enhancing cybersecurity.

So, fasten your seatbelts, fire up your computer, and get ready to explore the thrilling and essential world of ethical hacking and cybersecurity. As we embark on this educational voyage, remember that knowledge is power, and with great power comes great responsibility. Let's dive in and master the art of ethical hacking together.

BOOK 1
PENTESTING 101
A BEGINNER'S GUIDE TO ETHICAL HACKING

ROB BOTWRIGHT

Chapter 1: Introduction to Ethical Hacking

Ethical hacking, often referred to as penetration testing or white-hat hacking, is a crucial discipline within the field of cybersecurity. It entails authorized individuals, known as ethical hackers or penetration testers, attempting to find vulnerabilities and weaknesses in computer systems, networks, and applications, just as malicious hackers do, but with the noble aim of securing and fortifying these systems. The primary distinction between ethical hackers and malicious hackers lies in their intentions and the legality of their actions. Ethical hackers operate with the explicit permission of the system's owner or organization, and their activities are geared towards strengthening security, rather than causing harm or stealing sensitive information. The importance of ethical hacking has grown significantly in recent years due to the ever-increasing complexity and frequency of cyberattacks. As technology advances, so too does the sophistication of malicious hackers who constantly seek new ways to exploit weaknesses in digital systems, putting businesses, governments, and individuals at risk. To counter these threats, ethical hackers play a vital role in proactively identifying vulnerabilities before they can be exploited by cybercriminals. This proactive approach is essential in today's digital age, where data breaches and cyberattacks have the potential to cause massive financial losses and damage to an organization's reputation. The knowledge and skills of ethical hackers are in high demand, making it a lucrative and rewarding career path for those interested in cybersecurity. In this book, "Pentesting 101: A

Beginner's Guide to Ethical Hacking," we will explore the foundations of ethical hacking and provide you with the essential knowledge and tools to begin your journey in this exciting and dynamic field. Whether you are a newcomer to the world of cybersecurity or someone looking to transition into ethical hacking from another IT role, this book will serve as your comprehensive guide to getting started. We will start by delving into the basics of ethical hacking, including what it is, why it's essential, and the various ethical hacking methodologies and frameworks that professionals in this field use. You will gain an understanding of the ethical and legal aspects of hacking, learning how to obtain authorization to test and assess the security of systems and networks. We will also explore the critical concepts of vulnerability assessment and penetration testing, discussing their roles in identifying and mitigating security risks. To become an effective ethical hacker, you must become proficient in using a variety of tools and techniques. Throughout this book, we will introduce you to some of the most widely used ethical hacking tools and provide hands-on exercises to help you develop your skills. You will learn how to set up your own hacking environment, understand the mindset of a hacker, and practice scanning and enumeration techniques to identify potential vulnerabilities. As you progress through the chapters, we will cover essential topics such as exploiting vulnerabilities safely, web application security, wireless network hacking, and social engineering techniques. These skills will empower you to assess the security of networks, web applications, and even human behavior. Additionally, we will explore defensive strategies for ethical hackers, including ways to protect your own *systems and networks from potential attacks. Understanding the mindset and tactics of malicious hackers is crucial for effective defense. To provide you with practical insights, this book will present real-world scenarios and ethical hacking challenges that mimic the situations you may encounter in your career. These scenarios will help you apply your knowledge and skills in a practical context, honing your abilities to protect and secure systems effectively. By the time you complete this book, you will have a solid foundation in ethical hacking, enabling you to embark on a journey towards becoming a skilled and responsible ethical hacker. You will have the knowledge, tools, and ethical framework necessary to assess and improve the security posture of computer systems and networks, ultimately contributing to the safeguarding of sensitive data and information. Ethical hacking is a continuously evolving field, and staying up-to-date with the latest threats and countermeasures is essential for success. As such, this book will also provide guidance on further resources, certifications, and career development opportunities in the ethical hacking domain. Whether you aspire to become an ethical hacker or simply wish to enhance your cybersecurity knowledge, "Pentesting 101: A Beginner's Guide to Ethical Hacking" will serve as your comprehensive roadmap to success in this dynamic and vital discipline. Prepare to embark on a journey of exploration, learning, and empowerment, as we delve into the fascinating world of ethical hacking and the quest to secure the digital realm.*

Chapter 2: Setting Up Your Hacking Environment

When embarking on your journey into the world of ethical hacking, one of the crucial decisions you'll need to make is choosing the right operating system for your hacking environment. The choice of an operating system (OS) is fundamental as it lays the foundation for your entire hacking setup. Your chosen OS will determine which hacking tools and techniques are available to you, as well as how efficiently you can perform various tasks. As a beginner, you might be wondering which OS is best suited for ethical hacking and penetration testing. There are several options to consider, each with its advantages and limitations. One of the most popular choices among ethical hackers is Kali Linux. Kali Linux is a Debian-based distribution designed specifically for penetration testing and digital forensics. It comes pre-installed with a vast array of hacking tools and utilities, making it a convenient choice for newcomers to the field. Another option worth exploring is Parrot Security OS, which is also based on Debian and tailored for security professionals. Parrot Security OS offers a range of tools for penetration testing, cryptography, and privacy protection. Alternatively, you may opt for BlackArch Linux, an Arch Linux-based distribution that focuses on providing a vast repository of penetration testing tools. BlackArch Linux offers a rolling release model, ensuring that you have access to the latest tools and updates. While these are some of the popular Linux distributions for ethical hacking, you can also consider other options like BackBox and Pentoo, which cater to similar needs. However, the choice of your operating system isn't limited to Linux distributions alone. Some ethical hackers prefer using Unix-based systems like FreeBSD for specific tasks, as it offers robust security features and performance. Ultimately, the decision should be based on your personal preferences, goals, and the specific tasks you intend to perform. Before making your choice, it's essential to understand that ethical hacking often involves working in a command-line environment. This means you should be comfortable with using the terminal to execute commands and scripts. Linux-based operating systems, including Kali Linux and its variants, provide a familiar and powerful command-line interface, which is a valuable skill for ethical hackers. Additionally, consider the hardware requirements of your chosen operating system. Some Linux distributions, especially those loaded with numerous tools, may demand more system resources than others. Ensure that your computer or virtual machine meets the recommended specifications to run your OS efficiently. Virtualization is another aspect to consider. Many ethical hackers prefer using virtual machines (VMs) to create isolated and controlled environments for testing. VM software such as VirtualBox and VMware Player allows you to run multiple OS instances on a single physical machine. This approach can help you experiment with different operating systems and configurations without affecting your primary setup. When setting up your hacking environment, it's crucial to keep security and privacy in *mind. Always download your chosen operating system from official sources or trusted mirrors to avoid tampered or compromised versions. Verify the integrity of the downloaded ISO image by checking its cryptographic checksums, if provided. Additionally, consider using a virtual private network (VPN) to anonymize your internet connection and protect your identity while conducting ethical hacking activities. A VPN can help safeguard your online privacy and add an extra layer of security when interacting with potentially malicious systems or websites. Once you have selected the right operating system and ensured its integrity, it's time to install it on your computer or virtual machine. Follow the installation instructions provided by the OS distribution you've chosen. The installation process typically involves creating a bootable USB drive or DVD, booting from it, and following the on-screen prompts. During the installation, you will be asked to configure various settings, including language preferences, keyboard layout, and network settings. Make sure to choose options that align with your requirements and privacy considerations. After successfully installing your chosen operating system, you'll have access to a wide range of hacking tools and utilities. However, becoming proficient in ethical hacking requires more than just having the right tools at your disposal. It demands dedication, continuous learning, and a strong ethical framework. As you progress in your journey, you'll need to learn how to use these tools effectively, understand their capabilities and limitations, and apply them in real-world scenarios. Moreover, ethical hackers must adhere to strict ethical guidelines and legal boundaries. Obtaining proper authorization before conducting penetration tests and vulnerability assessments is essential. Unauthorized hacking attempts can have severe legal consequences, so it's crucial to always operate within the bounds of the law and with the consent of the system owner. In addition to ethical considerations, staying updated with the latest security threats and vulnerabilities is crucial for an ethical hacker. The cybersecurity landscape is constantly evolving, with new attack vectors and vulnerabilities emerging regularly. To stay ahead, ethical hackers must engage in continuous learning and professional development. One way to demonstrate your expertise and commitment to ethical hacking is by pursuing relevant certifications. Certifications such as Certified Ethical Hacker (CEH), CompTIA Security+, and Offensive Security Certified Professional (OSCP) are highly regarded in the industry. They not only validate your skills but also provide you with a structured curriculum and hands-on experience. Ethical hacking is a dynamic and challenging field that offers endless opportunities for learning and growth. By selecting the right operating system, understanding its features, and maintaining a strong ethical foundation, you can embark on a rewarding journey as an ethical hacker. Remember that ethical hacking is not about causing harm but about protecting and securing digital systems, making the digital world a safer place for everyone. Once you have chosen the appropriate operating system for your ethical hacking endeavors, the next crucial step is to* install and configure the necessary hacking tools and utilities. These tools will empower you to conduct various security assessments, vulnerability scans, and penetration tests. The process of installing and configuring hacking tools may seem intimidating at first, especially for beginners, but with proper guidance, it can be a manageable and rewarding experience. One of the advantages of using Linux-based operating systems like Kali Linux is that they come pre-loaded with a comprehensive suite of ethical hacking tools. This means you have many of the essential tools readily available right after the installation. However, it's important to keep in mind that the world of ethical hacking is vast, and there are numerous specialized tools for specific tasks. To ensure you have the right tools for your needs, it's a good practice to update the existing ones and add new ones to your arsenal. Updating your tools is essential because it ensures that you have the latest versions, which often include bug fixes, new features, and improved compatibility. To update the tools in your Linux distribution, you can use the package manager specific to your OS, such as apt for Debian-based systems or yum for Red Hat-based systems. For example, in Kali Linux, you can open a terminal and run the following command to update all installed packages: sqlCopy code

sudo apt update && sudo apt upgrade -y

This command fetches the latest package information from the repositories and upgrades all installed packages. It's important to execute these updates regularly to keep your hacking tools up to date. In addition to updating existing tools, you may want to install additional tools tailored to your specific ethical hacking tasks. These tools can range from network scanners and password-cracking utilities to wireless analysis and reverse engineering applications. To install new tools in Kali Linux, you can use the apt package manager or download and compile the source code manually, depending on the tool's availability. For example, if you want to install the Wireshark network protocol analyzer, you can use the following command: Copy code

```
sudo apt install wireshark -y
```

The '-y' flag is used to automatically answer 'yes' to any prompts that may appear during the installation process. This ensures a smooth and unattended installation. Once the tool is installed, you can typically access it from the terminal or the graphical user interface, depending on its nature. It's essential to thoroughly research and understand the tools you plan to use. Read the documentation, explore their features, and practice using them in a controlled environment. Ethical hacking tools can be potent, but they must be handled responsibly and with a clear understanding of their capabilities. Furthermore, consider organizing your tools effectively. Create directories or folders where you can categorize and store your tools based on their functionality. This organization will make it easier to locate and access the tools you need when conducting penetration tests or security assessments. Moreover, maintaining a clean and well-organized hacking environment will help you stay focused and efficient during your ethical hacking activities. In addition to installing and configuring hacking tools on your primary operating system, consider setting up virtual machines (VMs) or isolated environments for specific tasks or experiments. VMs provide a safe and controlled environment for testing and analyzing potentially harmful software or malware samples. Popular virtualization software like VirtualBox and VMware Player allows you to create and manage multiple virtual machines on a single physical host. You can install different operating systems on these VMs, allowing you to simulate various network scenarios or test your hacking skills on different platforms. Creating VMs for specific tasks, such as network analysis or malware analysis, can help you isolate your experiments and prevent any unintended consequences on your primary system. Additionally, snapshot functionality in virtualization software allows you to capture the current state of a VM and revert to it if something goes wrong during your experiments. This feature is valuable for maintaining a stable and secure hacking environment. Remember to allocate sufficient resources to your virtual machines, such as CPU cores, RAM, and storage, based on the requirements of your ethical hacking tasks. In addition to virtualization, containerization is another option to consider. Containers, powered by technologies like Docker, provide a lightweight and efficient way to package and deploy applications and services. You can create containers with specific tools and dependencies, making it easy to set up isolated environments for various hacking tasks. Containers are particularly useful when you need to work with specific tool versions or configurations. They offer a level of isolation while consuming fewer resources compared to traditional virtual machines. However, containers are typically more suitable for specific use cases, such as web application testing or development environments. As you install and configure hacking tools, it's essential to document your setup. Maintain a record of the tools you have installed, their versions, and any custom configurations or scripts you have implemented. Documentation serves as a valuable reference, especially when you need to rebuild your hacking environment or troubleshoot issues. Consider using version control systems like Git to manage your configurations and scripts, ensuring that you can track changes and collaborate with others effectively. Moreover, adopting a version control system can help you maintain consistency across your ethical hacking setup, whether you are working on a single machine or collaborating with a team. In summary, installing and configuring hacking tools is a crucial aspect of preparing your ethical hacking environment. Ensure that you keep your tools up to date, explore additional tools to expand your capabilities, and organize them effectively for easy access. Consider using virtual machines and containers for isolated testing environments, and document your setup for reference and collaboration. By taking these steps, you will be well-equipped to embark on your ethical hacking journey, ready to explore and secure digital systems responsibly and effectively.

Chapter 3: Understanding the Hacker Mindset

In the world of ethical hacking, one of the most valuable skills you can develop is the ability to think like an attacker. This mindset shift is crucial for identifying vulnerabilities and weaknesses in computer systems and networks. When you think like an attacker, you adopt a different perspective, focusing on how a malicious actor might exploit a system's weaknesses. By understanding the thought processes and tactics employed by hackers, you can proactively defend against potential threats. To think like an attacker, you must first cultivate a deep understanding of the motivations and goals that drive malicious actors. Malicious hackers often seek financial gain, access to sensitive information, or the ability to disrupt systems for various reasons. Understanding these motivations helps you anticipate the types of attacks that might target your systems. In addition to motivation, you need to consider the methods that hackers use to achieve their goals. Common attack vectors include exploiting software vulnerabilities, using social engineering tactics, and targeting weak or reused passwords. By familiarizing yourself with these attack vectors, you can better assess the potential risks to your systems. As you develop your attacker mindset, it's essential to stay informed about the latest security threats and attack techniques. The field of cybersecurity is dynamic, with new vulnerabilities and attack methods emerging regularly. Keeping up-to-date with current threats ensures that you can anticipate and respond to evolving security challenges effectively. One way to gain insights into the mind of an attacker is to study real-world attack scenarios and breach reports. Analyzing incidents that have occurred in the past can help you understand the tactics and techniques used by malicious hackers. Furthermore, participating in capture the flag (CTF) competitions and hackathons can provide hands-on experience in simulating and defending against attacks. These events offer a safe environment to hone your skills and apply your knowledge in a practical context. Another valuable exercise is to perform penetration testing and vulnerability assessments on your systems or lab environments. By attempting to breach your own defenses, you gain a deeper understanding of the vulnerabilities that exist and how they can be exploited. Ethical hackers use these assessments to uncover security weaknesses before malicious hackers can find and exploit them. Developing an attacker mindset also involves thinking critically and creatively. You must be able to identify potential weaknesses that others may overlook. Consider scenarios where attackers might leverage seemingly innocuous information or leverage social engineering tactics to gain access. By thinking creatively and exploring all possible attack vectors, you increase your chances of discovering and mitigating vulnerabilities. In addition to technical skills, an attacker mindset involves a strong ethical foundation. Ethical hackers must operate within the boundaries of the law and adhere to strict ethical guidelines. Obtaining proper authorization before conducting penetration tests and vulnerability assessments is paramount. Unauthorized hacking attempts can result in legal consequences, so it's essential to always seek permission when testing systems that are not your own. Furthermore, ethical hackers must maintain transparency and communicate their findings and recommendations to system owners or administrators. The goal is not to compromise systems but to identify and remediate vulnerabilities responsibly. Another aspect of thinking like an attacker is being persistent and thorough. Malicious hackers often use a combination of techniques and exploit multiple vulnerabilities to achieve their goals. As an ethical hacker, you must adopt a similar approach during penetration testing. Continuously probing for weaknesses and iterating through various attack vectors is essential for comprehensive security assessments. Thinking like an attacker also involves considering the potential consequences of a successful breach. You should assess the impact on data confidentiality, integrity, and availability. By understanding the potential fallout of a security incident, you can prioritize security measures and allocate resources effectively. Moreover, developing an attacker mindset means being proactive in your security efforts. Instead of waiting for vulnerabilities to be exploited, you actively seek out weaknesses and work to mitigate them. Regularly conducting security assessments and staying vigilant against emerging threats are essential components of a proactive approach. Additionally, ethical hackers must be adaptable and ready to pivot their strategies based on changing circumstances. Attackers are known for *their ability to adapt and evolve their tactics, so defenders must be equally flexible in response. Thinking like an attacker is not limited to technical skills; it encompasses a holistic approach to cybersecurity. It involves understanding the motivations, methods, and mindset of malicious hackers while maintaining a strong ethical foundation. By cultivating this attacker mindset, you can effectively identify and mitigate security vulnerabilities, helping to protect the systems and networks you are responsible for. Remember that ethical hacking is about securing digital environments responsibly and proactively, making the digital world safer for everyone.*

Understanding the motivations and goals of hackers is essential for anyone involved in the field of cybersecurity. Hackers, often portrayed as enigmatic figures operating in the shadows, have a wide range of motives for their actions. By delving into these motivations, we can gain valuable insights into the mindset of hackers and the types of threats they pose. One of the most common motivations for hacking is financial gain. Cybercriminals who seek monetary rewards exploit vulnerabilities in systems and networks to steal sensitive information, such as credit card numbers, personal data, or financial records. These attackers often operate covertly and employ sophisticated techniques to maximize their profits while avoiding detection. Financially motivated hackers may target individuals, businesses, or financial institutions, and their actions can lead to significant financial losses. Another prevalent motivation for hacking is ideological or political beliefs. Hacktivists, as they are often called, use their hacking skills to advance a particular cause, promote social or political change, or draw attention to specific issues. Their actions may include defacing websites, leaking sensitive information, or disrupting online services to convey their messages. Hacktivism blurs the line between traditional activism and cyberattacks, with hacktivists often operating in decentralized and loosely organized groups. Additionally, some hackers are motivated by the desire for notoriety or recognition within the hacking community. These individuals, known as "script kiddies" or "wannabe hackers," may lack advanced technical skills but seek attention and validation from their peers. They may use pre-packaged hacking tools or techniques created by others to carry out attacks, often with little understanding of the underlying technology. Although their motives differ from those of more seasoned hackers, script kiddies can still pose a threat to systems and networks. Another motivation for hacking is curiosity and the pursuit of knowledge. Some individuals are driven by a genuine interest in technology and cybersecurity, and they may engage in hacking activities to learn and experiment. These "white-hat hackers" or "ethical hackers" use their skills for constructive purposes, such as identifying vulnerabilities and helping organizations strengthen their security. Their actions are guided by a desire to improve cybersecurity rather than causing harm. While their motivations are generally positive, ethical hackers must operate within ethical and legal boundaries. Cyber espionage is another motivation behind hacking activities. State-sponsored hackers, intelligence agencies, and cybercriminal organizations may engage in espionage to gather sensitive information for political, military, or economic purposes. These attackers target governments, corporations, and other entities to steal classified or proprietary data, conduct surveillance, or gain a competitive advantage. The sophistication of cyber espionage campaigns can be exceptionally high, with attackers employing advanced techniques and maintaining persistence over extended periods. Hackers motivated by a desire for revenge or personal vendettas can pose a significant threat to specific individuals or organizations. These individuals may have a history of conflict or grievances and use hacking as a means to exact revenge or settle scores. Their actions can range from spreading false information to launching damaging cyberattacks. The "insider threat" is a related motivation, where individuals with legitimate access to an organization's systems and data abuse their privileges for personal gain or revenge. Hackers with insider knowledge can exploit their position to carry out attacks that may be difficult to detect. Some hackers are motivated by the challenge and thrill of hacking itself. Known as "black-hat hackers," these individuals enjoy the intellectual stimulation and excitement of breaking into systems and networks. They may view hacking as a game or a puzzle to solve, constantly seeking new ways to outsmart security measures. The challenge and adrenaline rush of successfully breaching security systems can be addictive to some black-hat hackers. Additionally, some hackers are motivated by a desire to test the security of systems and networks and help organizations identify and fix vulnerabilities. Known as "gray-hat hackers," they operate in a morally ambiguous space, often uncovering security flaws without permission but with the intention of alerting the affected parties. While their motives may be altruistic, gray-hat hackers may still face legal consequences for their actions if they operate without authorization. Understanding these various motivations and goals of hackers is essential for organizations and cybersecurity professionals tasked with defending against cyber threats. By recognizing the diverse range of hacker motivations, defenders can better assess and mitigate potential risks. It is important to remember that not all hackers are malicious, and some use their skills to protect and enhance cybersecurity. Ethical hacking, penetration testing, and vulnerability assessments are essential components of proactive security efforts. To effectively combat cyber threats, organizations and security practitioners must remain vigilant and adaptable, continuously evolving their defenses to counter the evolving tactics and motivations of hackers. Ultimately, a comprehensive approach to cybersecurity involves not only technical measures but also an understanding of the human factors that drive hacking behavior. By recognizing and addressing the motivations and goals of hackers, we can take significant steps toward creating a more secure digital landscape for individuals, businesses, and governments alike.

Chapter 4: Scanning and Enumeration Techniques

Network scanning is a fundamental component of ethical hacking and cybersecurity, allowing professionals to assess the security posture of networks, identify vulnerabilities, and gather critical information. Network scanning involves the systematic exploration of networked devices, systems, and services to discover their presence and assess their characteristics. It plays a vital role in understanding the network's layout, identifying potential entry points for attackers, and proactively mitigating security risks. There are several network scanning methods and techniques employed by ethical hackers and security professionals, each serving specific purposes and providing unique insights into network security. One of the most basic network scanning techniques is the use of ICMP (Internet Control Message Protocol) echo requests, commonly known as ping sweeps. Ping sweeps involve sending ICMP echo requests to a range of IP addresses to determine which hosts are online and responsive. This method is valuable for mapping the network and identifying active hosts. However, it may not provide detailed information about open ports or services running on the hosts. A more comprehensive approach to network scanning involves using port scanning techniques. Port scanning is the process of systematically checking the status of open and closed ports on a target host or network. Port scanners send packets to various ports on a target system and analyze the responses to determine whether the ports are open, closed, or filtered. The most well-known port scanning tool is Nmap (Network Mapper), which offers a wide range of scanning options and capabilities. Nmap allows ethical hackers to identify open ports, discover services running on those ports, and even determine the operating system of the target system. Nmap's flexibility and extensive feature set make it a preferred choice for many network scanning tasks. Additionally, ethical hackers often use stealthy scanning techniques, such as SYN scans (also known as half-open scans) and FIN scans, to avoid detection by intrusion detection systems (IDS) and firewall rules. These techniques send specially crafted packets to target ports, aiming to elicit specific responses that indicate whether a port is open. By using stealthy scans, ethical hackers can reduce the likelihood of alerting network defenders to their presence. In addition to port scanning, ethical hackers may perform banner grabbing to gather information about services running on open ports. Banner grabbing involves connecting to open ports and capturing the banners or headers sent by the services. These banners often reveal information about the service version and sometimes even provide clues about vulnerabilities. Banner grabbing can be conducted using tools like Telnet, Netcat, or specialized banner-grabbing tools. While network scanning can provide valuable insights, ethical hackers must conduct scans responsibly and within the bounds of legality and authorization. Unauthorized scanning of systems or networks can result in legal consequences and damage relationships with network owners. Therefore, it's crucial to obtain proper authorization before conducting any network scanning activities, whether it's in a controlled lab environment or a real-world assessment. Another important aspect of network scanning is the consideration of timing and scan intensity. Ethical hackers must balance the need for thorough scans with the desire to minimize disruption to network services and systems. Intensive or aggressive scans can overload network devices, causing service disruptions and raising alarms. As such, ethical hackers often employ techniques like slow scanning or randomization to avoid overwhelming target systems. Furthermore, ethical hackers must be aware of the legal and ethical implications of their scanning activities. Scanning systems or networks without permission can result in legal consequences and damage an individual's or organization's reputation. Therefore, obtaining explicit authorization from the system owner or administrator is essential before conducting any scanning activities. Moreover, ethical hackers should consider the potential impact of their scans on the availability and stability of the target network. A poorly planned or excessively aggressive scan can disrupt network services, leading to potential outages and affecting business operations. To mitigate these risks, ethical hackers often collaborate with network administrators to schedule scans during maintenance windows or non-critical periods. Additionally, it's crucial to monitor network traffic during scanning to detect any anomalies or unexpected behavior that may indicate a security incident. Regularly reviewing logs and analyzing the results of network *scans can help identify potential security issues and take appropriate actions to address them. In summary, network scanning is a vital aspect of ethical hacking and cybersecurity. It allows professionals to assess the security of networked systems, identify vulnerabilities, and gather critical information. By employing various scanning techniques and methods, ethical hackers can gain insights into network security, discover potential entry points for attackers, and proactively address security risks. However, ethical hackers must conduct scanning activities responsibly, obtain proper authorization, consider the impact on network availability, and adhere to legal and ethical guidelines. With a well-planned and careful approach, network scanning can be a valuable tool for strengthening the security of digital environments and protecting against cyber threats. Enumerating system information is a crucial phase in the ethical hacking process, providing valuable insights into the target system's configuration and potential vulnerabilities. This phase involves gathering detailed information about the target system's operating system, hardware, software, and network services. The gathered information serves as the foundation for further penetration testing and vulnerability assessment. Enumeration is the process of systematically extracting information from a target system or network. It involves querying various system components and services to discover details about their configurations and states. The primary goal of enumeration is to create a comprehensive profile of the target, which can then be analyzed to identify potential* weaknesses or areas for further investigation. One of the initial steps in system enumeration is determining the target's IP address and network range. This information is essential for identifying the scope of the assessment and selecting the appropriate tools and techniques. DNS (Domain Name System) enumeration can help identify hostnames, IP addresses, and subdomains associated with the target. Tools like nslookup or dig can be used to query DNS servers and retrieve information about the target's domain structure. Once the target's IP address and network range are known, the next step is to identify active hosts within the network. Ping sweeps and network scans can be employed to discover live systems and open ports. Nmap, as mentioned earlier, is a versatile tool that can perform both host discovery and port scanning to enumerate active hosts and open ports. As the enumeration process progresses, it's essential to gather detailed information about the target's operating system. Detecting the operating system version, patch level, and architecture helps ethical hackers identify potential vulnerabilities and exploits. OS fingerprinting techniques, such as banner grabbing and packet analysis, can be used to identify the target's operating system accurately. Once the operating system is identified, the enumeration process extends to uncovering additional system information. This includes gathering details about installed software, running services, and listening ports. Enumeration tools like enum4linux (for Windows systems), SNMP (Simple Network Management Protocol) queries, and banner-

grabbing tools can reveal valuable information about the software and services running on the target system. Ethical hackers often enumerate user accounts, groups, and permissions to assess the target's security posture. User enumeration can help identify valid user accounts, potentially weak passwords, and the existence of privileged accounts. Enumeration techniques vary based on the target system's platform. For Windows systems, tools like SMB enumeration tools, LDAP queries, and NetBIOS enumeration can be used to extract user and group information. On Unix-based systems, enumeration methods might involve querying the /etc/passwd file, reviewing user home directories, and examining the /etc/group file. Ethical hackers must exercise caution during user enumeration to avoid causing account lockouts or disruptions. Enumerating shares and file systems on networked systems is another critical aspect of system enumeration. Identifying open shares and their permissions can reveal sensitive data exposure or misconfigurations. Tools like SMBclient and enum4linux are commonly used for enumerating shares and file systems on Windows systems. Similarly, NFS (Network File System) enumeration tools can be employed to gather information about shared directories on Unix-based systems. Enumerating network services and their configurations is essential for assessing the target's security posture. Information about open ports, protocols in use, and service versions can help ethical hackers identify potential vulnerabilities and misconfigurations. Tools like Nmap, Nessus, and OpenVAS provide robust scanning and enumeration capabilities for network services. Ethical hackers also explore the target system's network shares, printers, and other networked resources. Enumeration techniques for network resources include SNMP queries, NetBIOS enumeration, and SNMP MIB (Management Information Base) exploration. For web applications and servers, enumerating directories, files, and web server configurations is a crucial step. Tools like Dirb, Dirbuster, and Nikto are commonly used for web enumeration to discover hidden directories, files, and potential vulnerabilities. Additionally, web server enumeration may involve examining HTTP response headers, identifying server technologies, and checking for misconfigurations. In addition to enumerating system information, ethical hackers must document their findings systematically. Detailed documentation helps create a clear and organized profile of the target system, making it easier to analyze and prioritize potential vulnerabilities. Maintaining comprehensive notes also aids in reporting findings to system owners or administrators, allowing them to address identified issues promptly. Moreover, ethical hackers must conduct enumeration activities responsibly and ethically. They should obtain proper authorization before scanning or enumerating target systems to ensure compliance with legal and ethical standards. Unauthorized enumeration can lead to legal consequences and damage relationships with network owners. Furthermore, ethical hackers should take measures to minimize the impact of enumeration on the target system's availability and performance. Careful planning and consideration of timing are crucial to avoid disrupting critical network services. In summary, system enumeration is a critical phase in ethical hacking, providing essential insights into a target system's configuration and potential vulnerabilities. By employing a variety of tools and techniques, ethical hackers can gather valuable information about operating systems, software, services, user accounts, and network resources. However, ethical hackers must conduct enumeration activities responsibly, obtain proper authorization, and minimize disruptions to the target system. Effective documentation of enumeration findings is also essential for subsequent analysis and reporting. Enumeration serves as the foundation for further penetration testing and vulnerability assessment, helping organizations strengthen their security posture and protect against cyber threats.

Chapter 5: Exploiting Vulnerabilities Safely

Identifying and prioritizing vulnerabilities is a critical step in the ethical hacking process, enabling organizations to strengthen their security posture and protect against potential threats. Vulnerabilities, which are weaknesses or flaws in systems, applications, or configurations, can be exploited by malicious actors to compromise the confidentiality, integrity, or availability of a target. Ethical hackers play a crucial role in identifying these vulnerabilities before they can be exploited, allowing organizations to proactively mitigate risks and safeguard their digital assets. The process of identifying vulnerabilities begins with a thorough assessment of the target system's security controls, configurations, and software. Ethical hackers examine various aspects of the system, including its operating system, network services, web applications, and infrastructure components. They employ a variety of techniques and tools to uncover potential weaknesses, such as vulnerability scanners, penetration testing, and manual code reviews. One common approach to vulnerability identification is the use of automated vulnerability scanning tools. These tools scan the target system for known vulnerabilities and misconfigurations by comparing its characteristics against a database of known security issues. Popular vulnerability scanning tools include Nessus, OpenVAS, and Qualys. These tools can identify vulnerabilities such as missing patches, weak passwords, and insecure configurations. While automated scanning tools are valuable for identifying common vulnerabilities, they may not catch all security issues, especially zero-day vulnerabilities or complex application-specific flaws. As a result, ethical hackers often complement automated scans with manual testing techniques. Manual testing involves in-depth examination and analysis of the target system, with a focus on identifying unique or custom vulnerabilities that automated tools may overlook. This may include reviewing source code, conducting penetration tests, and performing reverse engineering to uncover hidden vulnerabilities. Web applications are a common target for ethical hackers, as they often contain vulnerabilities that can be exploited to gain unauthorized access or compromise data. To identify web application vulnerabilities, ethical hackers use a variety of techniques, such as input validation testing, SQL injection testing, and cross-site scripting (XSS) testing. Web application scanning tools like OWASP ZAP and Burp Suite are commonly used for this purpose. In addition to assessing the technical aspects of a system, ethical hackers also examine the human and organizational factors that may contribute to vulnerabilities. Social engineering assessments, for example, involve attempting to manipulate individuals within an organization to reveal sensitive information or perform actions that compromise security. Identifying and prioritizing vulnerabilities is not only about finding flaws but also assessing their potential impact on the organization. Ethical hackers use risk assessment methodologies to evaluate the severity of vulnerabilities based on factors like the likelihood of exploitation, the potential impact on operations, and the value of the assets at risk. Common risk assessment frameworks include the Common Vulnerability Scoring System (CVSS) and the DREAD (Damage, Reproducibility,

Exploitability, Affected Users, and Discoverability) model. By assigning risk scores to vulnerabilities, ethical hackers can prioritize remediation efforts and focus on addressing the most critical issues first. For example, a critical vulnerability that could lead to a data breach may take precedence over a lower-severity issue that has a minimal impact on security. Once vulnerabilities are identified and prioritized, ethical hackers collaborate with organizations to develop a remediation plan. This plan outlines the steps and actions required to mitigate the identified vulnerabilities. It may include recommendations for applying security patches, reconfiguring systems, updating software, and enhancing security controls. Effective communication between ethical hackers and the organization's IT and security teams is crucial during this phase to ensure that remediation efforts are executed correctly and promptly. In some cases, the remediation plan may involve deploying temporary compensating controls to reduce the risk while a permanent solution is implemented. Ethical hackers often assist organizations in verifying the effectiveness of the remediation efforts through retesting. This ensures that the vulnerabilities have been successfully addressed and that the security measures put in place are effective. Vulnerability management is an ongoing process, as new vulnerabilities are continuously discovered, and systems evolve over time. Therefore, organizations should establish a proactive approach to identify, prioritize, and remediate vulnerabilities regularly. Regularly updating and patching systems, conducting security assessments, and staying informed about emerging threats are essential practices for maintaining a strong security posture. In summary, identifying and prioritizing vulnerabilities is a fundamental aspect of ethical hacking and cybersecurity. Ethical hackers employ a combination of automated scanning tools, manual testing techniques, and risk assessment methodologies to uncover weaknesses in systems and applications. Once vulnerabilities are identified, they work with organizations to develop remediation plans and prioritize the mitigation efforts based on the potential impact on security. Effective vulnerability management helps organizations protect their digital assets and reduce the risk of security breaches, ensuring the confidentiality, integrity, and availability of their systems and data. Exploiting vulnerabilities is a critical aspect of ethical hacking, as it allows professionals to demonstrate the potential impact of security flaws and help organizations strengthen their defenses. However, conducting exploitation activities in a real-world environment can have serious consequences, including service disruptions, data breaches, and legal repercussions. To avoid these risks, ethical hackers utilize lab environments that mimic real-world systems and networks while providing a controlled and safe testing environment. Setting up a lab environment for vulnerability exploitation involves several key steps to ensure safe and effective testing. The first step is to select suitable hardware and software for building the lab environment. Hardware requirements may include computers, servers, networking equipment, and virtualization technology. Virtualization platforms like VMware, VirtualBox, or Hyper-V are commonly used to create and manage virtual machines (VMs) within the lab. VMs allow ethical hackers to emulate different operating systems and network configurations, providing a diverse and realistic testing environment. Selecting the appropriate software is equally important, as it determines the range of vulnerabilities and configurations that can be tested. Common choices include various operating systems (e.g., Windows, Linux, macOS), web servers (e.g., Apache, Nginx), database systems (e.g., MySQL, PostgreSQL), and vulnerable applications. Next, ethical hackers need to design the lab network topology to replicate real-world scenarios. This involves defining network segments, configuring routers, switches, and firewalls, and implementing security controls such as intrusion detection systems (IDS) and firewalls. Creating a network layout that resembles the target environment allows for accurate vulnerability testing and exploitation. Ethical hackers should also establish a dedicated lab network to isolate testing activities from the production network, preventing unintended disruptions or exposure of sensitive data. Segmenting the lab network using virtual LANs (VLANs) or separate physical network adapters can help achieve this isolation. Once the lab environment is set up, ethical hackers must populate it with target systems and services that mirror those found in the real world. This includes configuring VMs with various operating systems and installing software and applications that may be susceptible to known vulnerabilities. Vulnerable applications like web content management systems, e-commerce platforms, or forum software can be added to simulate real-world web application vulnerabilities. To make the lab environment as realistic as possible, ethical hackers should keep systems and software up to date with security patches and updates. While lab environments aim to replicate real-world scenarios, they should also include *additional security measures to maintain control and prevent unintended consequences. For example, deploying network-based IDS and IPS (Intrusion Prevention System) solutions can help monitor and mitigate potential threats during testing. Implementing network segmentation and access controls ensures that testing activities are confined to the lab environment. Additionally, ethical hackers can create backups of the lab environment to restore it to a known good state in case of accidental damage or security incidents. Once the lab environment is configured and secured, ethical hackers can begin the process of vulnerability exploitation. This typically involves identifying and selecting specific vulnerabilities to target. Vulnerabilities can be discovered through various means, including vulnerability scanning, manual testing, and research on known security issues. Common sources of vulnerability information include the National Vulnerability Database (NVD), the Common Vulnerabilities and Exposures (CVE) database, and security advisories from software vendors. Once a vulnerability is identified, ethical hackers need to understand its characteristics and potential impact to determine if it is suitable for exploitation. This assessment considers factors like the severity of the vulnerability, the ease of exploitation, and the potential consequences of a successful attack. Ethical hackers should prioritize vulnerabilities based on their impact and relevance to the target environment. After selecting a vulnerability for exploitation, ethical hackers create a detailed plan of attack. This plan outlines the specific steps and techniques that will be used to exploit the vulnerability. It may include writing or customizing exploit code, configuring attack tools, and defining the objectives of the exploitation. Ethical hackers should thoroughly test their exploits in the lab environment to ensure they work as intended and minimize the risk of unintended damage. Before executing any exploitation activities, ethical hackers should obtain proper authorization from the organization that owns the lab environment. This authorization ensures that testing activities are conducted legally and ethically, reducing the risk of legal repercussions. Once authorization is granted, ethical hackers can proceed with the exploitation phase, carefully following the plan of attack. Throughout the exploitation process, ethical hackers should maintain strict documentation of their activities, recording the steps taken, the tools used, and the results obtained. This documentation is essential for analysis, reporting, and auditing purposes. It provides a detailed account of the exploitation process and helps organizations understand the impact of vulnerabilities and the need for remediation. During exploitation, ethical hackers should continuously monitor the lab environment for unexpected behaviors, system crashes, or unintended consequences. Vulnerability exploitation can sometimes have unforeseen outcomes, so vigilance is crucial. Upon successful exploitation, ethical hackers may gain unauthorized access to systems, compromise data, or demonstrate the potential impact of the vulnerability. Once the exploitation phase is complete, ethical hackers should report their findings and provide recommendations for remediation to the organization that authorized the testing. This report details the vulnerabilities identified, the exploitation process, and the potential risks to the organization. It also outlines recommended actions to mitigate the vulnerabilities and improve security. In summary, safely exploiting vulnerabilities in a lab environment is a fundamental aspect of ethical hacking, allowing professionals to assess and demonstrate the impact of security flaws without exposing real-world systems to risk. By carefully designing and securing the lab environment, selecting appropriate hardware and software, and following ethical guidelines, ethical hackers can conduct effective vulnerability exploitation activities while minimizing potential harm. These activities ultimately help organizations identify and remediate vulnerabilities, enhancing their overall security posture and protecting against real-world cyber threats.*

Chapter 6: Web Application Security Basics

Web applications have become an integral part of our digital lives, providing functionality and interactivity across a wide range of online platforms. However, with their widespread use comes an increased risk of security vulnerabilities that can be exploited by malicious actors to compromise sensitive data, disrupt services, or gain unauthorized access. Understanding common web application vulnerabilities is crucial for developers, security professionals, and ethical hackers to protect against potential threats. One of the most prevalent web application vulnerabilities is Cross-Site Scripting (XSS). XSS occurs when an application includes untrusted data in a web page, allowing an attacker to inject malicious scripts that are executed in the context of the user's browser. These scripts can steal session cookies, perform actions on behalf of the user, or deface web pages. To prevent XSS, developers should validate and sanitize user inputs, escape output, and implement security headers like Content Security Policy (CSP). Another significant web application vulnerability is SQL Injection (SQLi), where attackers exploit poorly sanitized user inputs to inject malicious SQL queries into database queries. This can lead to unauthorized access to the database, data leakage, or even database manipulation. To mitigate SQL Injection, developers should use parameterized queries or prepared statements, employ input validation, and follow the principle of least privilege in database access. Cross-Site Request Forgery (CSRF) is a vulnerability that allows attackers to trick users into performing unwanted actions on a web application without their consent. This occurs when an attacker forges a request that appears legitimate, causing the user's browser to execute actions on the target site on behalf of the attacker. Developers can prevent CSRF by using anti-CSRF tokens, verifying the origin of requests, and ensuring that sensitive actions require authentication. Another web application vulnerability is Security Misconfigurations, which occur when developers or administrators overlook security settings and leave applications, servers, or databases in insecure states. Attackers can exploit misconfigurations to gain unauthorized access, steal sensitive data, or disrupt services. To prevent security misconfigurations, organizations should follow security best practices, conduct regular security assessments, and use automated scanning tools to identify vulnerabilities. Insecure Deserialization is a vulnerability where attackers manipulate serialized data to execute arbitrary code, gain unauthorized access, or perform other malicious actions. Developers can mitigate insecure deserialization by validating and sanitizing incoming data, using safe deserialization libraries, and implementing proper input validation. Another common web application vulnerability is Broken Authentication, which occurs when authentication and session management are not implemented securely. Attackers can exploit these flaws to gain unauthorized access to user accounts, impersonate users, or bypass authentication mechanisms. Developers should use secure authentication methods, implement session management best practices, and enforce strong password policies to prevent broken authentication. Sensitive Data Exposure is a vulnerability where sensitive *information, such as passwords or financial data, is not adequately protected. Attackers can exploit this vulnerability to steal confidential data and use it for malicious purposes. To prevent sensitive data exposure, developers should use strong encryption for data at rest and in transit, follow data protection regulations, and limit data exposure to only what is necessary. Broken Access Control is a vulnerability that occurs when developers fail to enforce proper access controls, allowing unauthorized users to access restricted resources or perform privileged actions. Attackers can exploit this vulnerability to gain unauthorized access to other users' accounts, manipulate data, or perform administrative actions. To mitigate broken access control, developers should implement role-based access control (RBAC), enforce proper authorization checks, and conduct thorough security testing. Security researchers and organizations have identified and categorized these common web application vulnerabilities as part of ongoing efforts to improve web security. The Open Web Application Security Project (OWASP), for example, maintains the OWASP Top Ten, which is a list of the most critical web application security risks. By staying informed about these vulnerabilities and following best practices for secure coding and web application development, organizations can reduce their risk of falling victim to web-based attacks. Security professionals and ethical hackers can also leverage this knowledge to assess and secure web applications, proactively identifying and remediating vulnerabilities before they can be exploited by malicious actors. In summary, web application vulnerabilities pose a significant threat to the security and integrity of online services and data. Understanding and addressing common web application vulnerabilities is essential for developers, security professionals, and ethical hackers to protect against potential threats. By following best practices, conducting security assessments, and staying informed about emerging risks, organizations can enhance the security of their web applications and provide a safer online experience for users.*

Web application testing is a critical part of ensuring the security and functionality of web-based software. As the digital landscape continues to evolve, web applications have become a primary target for cyberattacks. Effective web application testing methodologies are essential to identify and mitigate vulnerabilities and flaws in web applications. These methodologies help organizations maintain the confidentiality, integrity, and availability of their systems and data. One widely adopted approach to web application testing is the use of the Open Web Application Security Project (OWASP) Testing Guide. The OWASP Testing Guide provides a comprehensive framework for testing web applications and is a valuable resource for security professionals and ethical hackers. It covers a wide range of testing techniques and provides guidance on how to assess security controls, identify vulnerabilities, and verify compliance with security best practices. The OWASP Testing Guide outlines various phases of web application testing, including information gathering, configuration management testing, authentication testing, session management testing, and business logic testing. Each phase focuses on specific aspects of web application security and provides detailed instructions and testing scenarios. Information gathering is an essential initial phase in web application testing. It involves collecting information about the target application, such as its architecture, technologies used, and potential entry points for attackers. Tools like automated scanners, web crawlers, and network reconnaissance techniques can assist in information gathering. Configuration management testing assesses the security of application configurations. This phase aims to identify misconfigurations that could expose vulnerabilities or weaken security controls. Common configuration issues include default credentials, unnecessary services running, and insecure settings. Authentication testing evaluates the effectiveness of the authentication mechanisms used by the web application. Testers attempt to bypass authentication, perform password guessing attacks, and assess the strength of password policies. Session management testing examines how the application manages user sessions and tokens. Testers check for session fixation vulnerabilities, session hijacking, and inadequate session timeouts. Business logic testing focuses on the application's core functionality and logic. Testers attempt to manipulate inputs, perform parameter tampering, and test for logical flaws that could lead to unauthorized access or data exposure. Another important web application testing methodology is the Application Security Verification Standard (ASVS) created by the OWASP organization. The ASVS provides a set of security requirements for designing, building, and testing modern web applications and web services. It offers a comprehensive framework for ensuring that web applications are secure and resilient to common attacks. The ASVS is organized into three levels of verification, with each level addressing different security requirements.

Level 1 focuses on the most critical and fundamental security controls that should be in place for all web applications. These controls include authentication, session management, access control, and input validation. Level 2 adds more advanced security controls that are relevant for web applications with higher security requirements. These controls include cryptographic mechanisms, secure file uploads, and secure coding practices. Level 3 includes the most rigorous security requirements and is suitable for applications with extremely high security needs. These requirements cover areas like advanced session management, client-side security, and secure deployment. Web application testing methodologies also include the use of automated vulnerability scanners and penetration testing. Automated scanners, such as Burp Suite, Nessus, and OWASP ZAP, are tools that can quickly identify common vulnerabilities like Cross-Site Scripting (XSS), SQL Injection, and CSRF. Penetration testing, on the other hand, involves skilled testers manually probing for vulnerabilities, simulating real-world attack scenarios, and identifying security weaknesses that automated tools may miss. Both automated scanning and penetration testing are valuable components of a comprehensive web application testing strategy. Security professionals and ethical hackers should perform regular security assessments, such as vulnerability scanning and penetration testing, to identify and remediate vulnerabilities in web applications. Regular testing helps ensure that web applications remain secure in the face of evolving threats and changing application landscapes. Additionally, organizations should integrate security testing into their software development lifecycle

(SDLC) to address vulnerabilities early in the development process. This proactive approach helps reduce the cost and effort required to fix vulnerabilities and promotes a security-first mindset within development teams. It's essential to conduct thorough security testing at each stage of the SDLC, from design and development to testing and deployment. In summary, web application testing methodologies play a vital role in identifying and mitigating security vulnerabilities in web-based software. Security professionals and ethical hackers rely on frameworks like the OWASP Testing Guide and the ASVS to guide their testing efforts and ensure comprehensive coverage of security controls. Automated scanning tools and manual penetration testing further enhance the testing process by identifying vulnerabilities and weaknesses in web applications. Regular security assessments and integration of security testing into the SDLC are key practices for maintaining the security and resilience of web applications in an ever-evolving threat landscape.

Chapter 7: Wireless Network Hacking

Wi-Fi networks have become an integral part of our daily lives, providing wireless connectivity for a wide range of devices and applications. However, the convenience of Wi-Fi comes with security challenges, as wireless networks are susceptible to various vulnerabilities and attacks. Understanding Wi-Fi security protocols and their weaknesses is essential for securing wireless networks and protecting sensitive information. One of the most common Wi-Fi security protocols is WEP (Wired Equivalent Privacy), which was introduced in the early days of Wi-Fi. WEP uses a shared key to encrypt data transmitted over the wireless network, but it has several significant weaknesses. One of the main weaknesses of WEP is its reliance on a static encryption key that is shared among all devices on the network. This key is vulnerable to interception and can be easily cracked using readily available tools, making WEP an insecure choice for Wi-Fi security. Another weakness of WEP is its use of a small Initialization Vector (IV) space, which allows attackers to predict and analyze IVs, facilitating the recovery of the encryption key. To address the weaknesses of WEP, Wi-Fi security standards evolved to WPA (Wi-Fi Protected Access) and its successor, WPA2. WPA introduced dynamic encryption keys through the use of Temporal Key Integrity Protocol (TKIP) and improved authentication mechanisms. However, WPA still had its own weaknesses, such as susceptibility to brute force attacks on weak passphrases. WPA2, on the other hand, addressed many of these vulnerabilities and became the de facto standard for secure Wi-Fi networks. WPA2 uses the Advanced Encryption Standard (AES) for data encryption, which is much stronger than the encryption used in WEP and WPA. AES encryption is considered highly secure and is resistant to known attacks. Despite its strong encryption, WPA2 has its own set of vulnerabilities, with one of the most notable being the KRACK (Key Reinstallation Attacks) vulnerability. KRACK allows an attacker to intercept and manipulate data by exploiting weaknesses in the WPA2 handshake process. While patches were developed to mitigate KRACK, this vulnerability highlighted the need for continued vigilance in Wi-Fi security. As technology advances, so do the security protocols designed to protect Wi-Fi networks. WPA3 is the latest Wi-Fi security protocol, offering significant improvements in security compared to its predecessors. WPA3 introduces several enhancements, including stronger encryption, protection against brute force attacks on weak passwords, and improved security for open networks. One of the key features of WPA3 is the Simultaneous Authentication of Equals (SAE) handshake, which replaces the vulnerable WPA2 handshake. SAE provides more robust protection against offline dictionary attacks and brute force attacks on the pre-shared key. Additionally, WPA3 encrypts data traffic even if the pre-shared key used for authentication is weak, further enhancing security. While WPA3 offers improved security, it's important to note that the adoption of WPA3 may take time, and many Wi-Fi devices still rely on WPA2. Therefore, it's essential for users to be aware of the security protocol in use on their Wi-Fi networks and ensure that their devices and routers are updated with the latest security patches. Beyond the specific security protocols, Wi-Fi networks can also be vulnerable to other types of attacks and weaknesses. One common vulnerability is the use of default credentials on routers and access points. Many users fail to change the default usernames and passwords on their Wi-Fi devices, making them easy targets for attackers. Default credentials are often well-documented and can be easily exploited to gain unauthorized access to the network. To mitigate this weakness, users should always change default login credentials on their Wi-Fi devices and choose strong, unique passwords. Another Wi-Fi vulnerability is the risk of rogue access points. Attackers can set up rogue access points with names similar to legitimate networks, tricking users into connecting to them. Once connected, attackers can intercept traffic, steal information, or launch further attacks. To defend against rogue access points, users should verify the network they are connecting to, avoid public Wi-Fi networks for sensitive transactions, and use Virtual Private Networks (VPNs) for added security. Wi-Fi networks are also vulnerable to eavesdropping attacks, where attackers intercept and monitor wireless communications. Encryption, such as that provided by WPA2 or WPA3, helps protect against eavesdropping by encrypting data in transit. However, open Wi-Fi networks, which lack encryption, are particularly susceptible to eavesdropping. Users should exercise caution when using open Wi-Fi networks and avoid transmitting sensitive information unless using additional encryption methods. Man-in-the-Middle (MitM) attacks are another concern for Wi-Fi security. In a MitM attack, an attacker intercepts and alters communication between two parties without their knowledge. MitM attacks can occur on both encrypted and *unencrypted Wi-Fi networks. To mitigate MitM attacks, users should regularly update their devices and use security features like HTTPS for secure web browsing. Wi-Fi security is a dynamic field, with new vulnerabilities and attacks emerging as technology evolves. It's crucial for users and organizations to stay informed about the latest security threats and best practices for securing Wi-Fi networks. Regularly updating devices, using strong passwords, enabling encryption, and being cautious when connecting to unfamiliar networks are essential steps in maintaining Wi-Fi security. Additionally, monitoring network traffic and staying vigilant for signs of unauthorized access or unusual activity can help detect and respond to security incidents promptly. In summary, Wi-Fi security protocols have evolved significantly over the years, from the insecure WEP to the more robust WPA2 and the even stronger WPA3. Each protocol addresses vulnerabilities and weaknesses present in its predecessors, but new threats continue to emerge. Users and organizations must remain proactive in securing their Wi-Fi networks by implementing the latest security measures, using strong passwords, and being vigilant against evolving threats. Wi-Fi networks have become ubiquitous, providing wireless connectivity for devices and enabling convenient internet access. However, securing Wi-Fi networks is crucial to prevent unauthorized access and protect sensitive data. One common method used by attackers to compromise Wi-Fi networks is cracking Wi-Fi passwords. Cracking Wi-Fi passwords allows attackers to gain unauthorized access to a network and potentially intercept or manipulate data traffic. Understanding the techniques used by attackers to crack Wi-Fi passwords is* essential for network administrators and security professionals to defend against such threats. One of the most well-known Wi-Fi password cracking techniques is brute force attacks. Brute force attacks involve attempting all possible combinations of characters until the correct password is discovered. Attackers use specialized tools that automate the process of trying different combinations, making it feasible to crack weak or poorly chosen passwords. To defend against brute force attacks, users and organizations should use strong, complex passwords that are resistant to dictionary-based attacks. Another common technique used to crack Wi-Fi passwords is dictionary attacks. In a dictionary attack, attackers use a predefined list of words, phrases, or common passwords to guess the network's password. This method is more efficient than brute force attacks because it narrows down the possibilities, focusing on likely passwords. To counter dictionary attacks, users should avoid using easily guessable passwords, such as "password" or "123456," and choose unique and complex combinations of characters. Attackers also employ online and offline attacks to crack Wi-Fi passwords. Online attacks involve directly targeting the network by attempting to log in with guessed passwords. In contrast, offline attacks capture the encrypted handshake between a device and the access point and then attempt to crack the password offline. The offline approach is more challenging for defenders to detect, as it doesn't rely on repeated login attempts. To protect against online and offline attacks, users should implement strong encryption protocols like WPA3, which are resistant to known attacks. Cracking Wi-Fi passwords can be further complicated by the use of salted password hashes. Salted hashes add random data to passwords before hashing, making it more difficult for attackers to precompute hashes for common passwords. This practice enhances password security and makes password cracking more challenging. Network administrators should consider implementing salted hashes to protect user passwords stored on authentication servers. Wi-Fi Protected Setup (WPS) is another feature that can introduce vulnerabilities when not properly configured. WPS allows users to easily connect devices to a Wi-Fi network by entering a PIN or pushing a button on the router. However, WPS is susceptible to brute force attacks, where attackers try all possible PIN combinations until they find the correct one. To secure Wi-Fi networks, users should disable WPS or ensure that it is configured securely with strong PINs. Rainbow tables are precomputed tables of password hashes that attackers use to quickly look up hashes and find corresponding passwords. These tables can accelerate the password cracking process and are a concern for network security. To mitigate the risk of rainbow table attacks, organizations should implement password salting and use strong hashing algorithms. Wireless networks can also be vulnerable to rogue access points, which are unauthorized devices that mimic legitimate Wi-Fi networks. Rogue access points can trick users into connecting to them, allowing attackers to intercept traffic or launch attacks. To defend against rogue access points, organizations should regularly scan for unauthorized devices and employ wireless intrusion detection systems (WIDS) to monitor network activity. Wi-Fi networks using outdated encryption protocols like WEP or WPA should upgrade to more secure standards like WPA3. Security professionals can use penetration testing tools and techniques to assess the security of Wi-Fi networks. Penetration testing helps identify vulnerabilities and weaknesses in network configurations, encryption, and access controls. It provides valuable insights that enable organizations to strengthen their Wi-Fi security. In summary, cracking Wi-Fi passwords and gaining unauthorized access to Wi-Fi networks pose significant security risks. Attackers use various techniques, such as brute force attacks, dictionary attacks, and online/offline attacks, to crack Wi-Fi passwords and compromise networks. To defend against these threats, users and organizations should implement strong, unique passwords, disable insecure features like WPS, and use the latest encryption standards like WPA3. Regular security assessments and monitoring are essential to maintaining Wi-Fi network security and protecting sensitive data from unauthorized access. By understanding the techniques used by attackers and implementing robust security measures, network administrators and security professionals can reduce the risk of Wi-Fi password cracking and safeguard wireless networks effectively.

Chapter 8: Social Engineering and Phishing

Social engineering is a form of manipulation and deception used by malicious individuals to exploit human psychology and gain unauthorized access to information, systems, or physical locations. It is a non-technical approach to hacking that relies on the human element as its primary target. Understanding social engineering techniques is essential for individuals and organizations to defend against this type of attack. One common social engineering technique is phishing, where attackers impersonate trusted entities, such as banks, email providers, or coworkers, to trick victims into revealing sensitive information like login credentials or financial details. Phishing often involves sending deceptive emails with links to fraudulent websites or malicious attachments. To protect against phishing, individuals should be cautious when clicking on links or opening attachments from unknown or suspicious sources and verify the legitimacy of requests for sensitive information. Another social engineering technique is pretexting, where attackers create a fabricated scenario or pretext to obtain information from the victim. They may impersonate authority figures, tech support personnel, or colleagues and request information under the guise of a legitimate need. Pretexting can be used to gain access to personal or corporate data, and individuals should be vigilant when sharing sensitive information with unfamiliar contacts. Baiting is a social engineering technique that entices victims with an offer or incentive to download malicious software or disclose sensitive information. Attackers may leave infected USB drives, CDs, or files in public places, hoping that someone will take the bait. To protect against baiting, individuals should avoid using unknown storage devices and be cautious of unsolicited offers or free downloads. Quid pro quo is a technique where attackers offer a service or benefit in exchange for information or access. For example, an attacker may claim to be an IT technician offering free software or technical support in exchange for login credentials. Individuals should never provide login credentials or sensitive information to anyone in exchange for services without proper verification. Tailgating, or piggybacking, is a physical social engineering technique where attackers follow authorized individuals into secure areas or buildings without proper access. Attackers may exploit a victim's courtesy or lack of attention to gain unauthorized entry. To prevent tailgating, individuals should be cautious about holding secure doors open for strangers and should challenge unfamiliar individuals attempting to enter restricted areas. Impersonation is another social engineering technique where attackers pose as someone the victim knows or trusts. This could involve impersonating coworkers, friends, or family members in person, on the phone, or through digital communication. Individuals should verify the identity of individuals making unusual or suspicious requests. Preventing social engineering attacks often involves education and awareness. Employees should receive training to recognize common social engineering tactics and understand the importance of verifying requests for sensitive information. Organizations can implement policies and procedures for handling sensitive information and reporting suspected social engineering attempts. Pharming is a social engineering technique where attackers manipulate the domain name system (DNS) to redirect users to fraudulent websites without their knowledge. Victims may enter their login credentials or financial information on these fake sites, unknowingly providing them to attackers. To protect against pharming, individuals should use secure, reputable DNS servers, and organizations should implement DNSSEC (Domain Name System Security Extensions) to prevent DNS tampering. Vishing, or voice phishing, is a social engineering technique that involves using phone calls to impersonate legitimate organizations or authorities to extract sensitive information from victims. Attackers may pose as bank representatives, government agencies, or tech support personnel to trick victims into revealing personal or financial information. To defend against vishing, individuals should verify the identity of callers and avoid sharing sensitive information over the phone. Online personas and social media profiles can be manipulated by attackers to gather information and build trust with potential victims. Attackers may create fake online identities and interact with individuals to collect personal details or exploit relationships. Individuals should be cautious about sharing personal information online and verify the identities of online contacts. Social engineering techniques are continually evolving, and *attackers often use a combination of tactics to exploit human psychology and trust. Individuals and organizations must remain vigilant and stay informed about emerging threats. Regularly updating security policies, providing training and awareness programs, and implementing strong authentication and access control measures are essential steps in defending against social engineering attacks. In summary, social engineering techniques target human psychology and trust to manipulate individuals into revealing sensitive information or granting unauthorized access. Understanding these tactics and implementing security measures and awareness programs are crucial for individuals and organizations to defend against social engineering attacks effectively. By recognizing the signs of manipulation and maintaining a cautious approach to requests for sensitive information, individuals can protect themselves from falling victim to social engineering schemes. Organizations can strengthen their defenses by educating employees, implementing robust security policies, and continuously monitoring for suspicious activity. Phishing campaigns are deceptive and malicious attempts to manipulate individuals into divulging sensitive information, such as login credentials, financial details, or personal data. While phishing is widely recognized as a threat, it's important to understand the tactics used by attackers to design and execute effective phishing campaigns. By comprehending the methods employed by malicious actors, individuals and organizations can better protect themselves against these fraudulent schemes. One fundamental aspect of designing a phishing campaign is the creation of a convincing pretext or scenario. Attackers often impersonate trusted entities, such as banks, email providers, or colleagues, to establish credibility and lure victims into taking action. The pretext should be plausible and relatable to the target audience to maximize the chances of success. Attackers may leverage current events, create a sense of urgency, or exploit individuals' fears and concerns to craft convincing pretexts. Another critical element in a phishing campaign is the selection of the attack vector. Attackers can choose from various attack vectors, including email, text messages, social media, instant messaging, or even phone calls. The choice of attack vector depends on the target audience, the pretext used, and the attacker's objectives. For example, email phishing is prevalent because it allows attackers to reach a large audience and deliver malicious content discreetly. Attackers may also employ spear phishing, a targeted approach that customizes the message and pretext for specific individuals or organizations. Crafting a compelling message is essential in a phishing campaign. Attackers use social engineering techniques to manipulate emotions, curiosity, or fear to encourage victims to take action. The message should be concise, clear, and designed to evoke the desired response, such as clicking a link, downloading an attachment, or providing sensitive information. Attackers often employ psychological tactics, such as urgency or scarcity, to persuade victims to act quickly without thinking critically. Phishing emails may include compelling* subject lines, appealing offers, or alarming warnings to increase their effectiveness. The use of malicious URLs or attachments is a common tactic in phishing campaigns. Attackers create fraudulent websites that mimic legitimate ones to steal login credentials or financial information. These fake websites often have domain names or URLs that closely resemble those of trusted organizations. To avoid detection, attackers may use URL shorteners or exploit URL redirection to hide the true destination. Attachments in phishing emails may contain malware or malicious scripts that exploit vulnerabilities in software or systems. To protect against phishing, individuals should be cautious when clicking on links or downloading attachments from unfamiliar or suspicious sources. Attackers often use obfuscation techniques to evade detection by security filters. Obfuscation involves disguising the malicious content in a way that makes it challenging for automated security systems to detect. This may include encoding or encrypting the payload, using image-based text, or embedding malicious scripts within seemingly harmless documents. To detect obfuscated content, organizations should employ advanced email security solutions and regularly update their security measures. Email spoofing is another technique used to deceive recipients. Attackers manipulate email headers to make it appear as though the email originates from a trusted source. Spoofed emails may display familiar sender names, email addresses, or domain names. To combat email spoofing, organizations can implement email authentication protocols like SPF (Sender Policy

Framework), DKIM (DomainKeys Identified Mail), and DMARC (Domain-based Message Authentication, Reporting, and Conformance). Attackers often leverage psychological manipulation to exploit human emotions and decision-making processes. For example, they may use fear tactics, such as threatening account suspension or legal consequences, to pressure victims into taking immediate action. Alternatively, they may promise enticing rewards or prizes to entice recipients to click on malicious links or provide personal information. To counteract these tactics, individuals should remain calm and verify the legitimacy of the communication independently. Phishing campaigns can also employ social engineering tactics to gather information about targets. Attackers may pose as colleagues, acquaintances, or tech support personnel to build trust and extract sensitive data. These tactics rely on human psychology and the natural tendency to trust individuals with familiar or authoritative roles. Individuals should verify the identity of individuals making unusual or sensitive requests and exercise caution when sharing personal or financial information. Social media profiling is a technique used to gather information about potential targets. Attackers may create fake online personas and interact with individuals to collect personal details or exploit relationships. These profiles can appear convincing and relatable, making it easier to manipulate individuals into revealing information. To protect against social media profiling, individuals should limit the information shared online and verify the identity of online contacts. To execute a phishing campaign successfully, attackers often conduct reconnaissance to gather information about potential targets. They may use open-source intelligence (OSINT) techniques to collect data from publicly available sources, such as social media profiles, company websites, or public records. This information helps attackers tailor their pretexts and messages to increase their chances of success. To defend against reconnaissance, individuals should be cautious about the information they share publicly and regularly review their online presence for potential vulnerabilities. Phishing campaigns often target specific individuals or organizations. Spear phishing is a targeted approach that customizes the message and pretext for a specific audience. Attackers conduct research to gather information about their targets and craft personalized messages to increase the likelihood of success. These messages may reference specific individuals, projects, or events to appear more convincing. To defend against spear phishing, individuals and organizations should implement strong email security measures, educate employees about the risks, and encourage a culture of cybersecurity awareness. The success of a phishing campaign often hinges on the attacker's ability to evade detection and bypass security measures. To do this, attackers may use evasion techniques, such as using multiple redirections, employing URL shorteners, or using domain names that have not been blacklisted. Additionally, attackers may regularly change their tactics and infrastructure to stay ahead of security defenses. Organizations should employ advanced email *security solutions that use machine learning and behavior analysis to detect evolving phishing threats. Phishing campaigns can have severe consequences for individuals and organizations, including data breaches, financial losses, and reputational damage. To protect against phishing, individuals should remain vigilant, verify the legitimacy of messages and requests, and report suspicious activity to their organization's security team. Organizations should invest in robust email security solutions, conduct regular security awareness training, and implement security policies and procedures to mitigate the risks associated with phishing. In summary, understanding the tactics used by attackers to design and execute phishing campaigns is crucial for individuals and organizations to defend against these deceptive and malicious attempts. By recognizing the techniques employed in phishing, individuals can become more resilient to manipulation and better equipped to protect themselves and their organizations from falling victim to phishing schemes. By combining education, awareness, and advanced security measures, organizations can significantly reduce their susceptibility to phishing attacks and enhance their overall cybersecurity posture.*

Chapter 9: Defensive Strategies for Ethical Hackers

Effective security controls are essential to protect information systems, networks, and data from a wide range of threats and vulnerabilities. Implementing these controls is a fundamental aspect of cybersecurity, helping organizations safeguard their assets and maintain the confidentiality, integrity, and availability of critical information. This chapter explores the key principles and practices for implementing effective security controls. One of the foundational principles of security control implementation is the principle of defense in depth. This principle emphasizes the use of multiple layers of security controls to create a robust and resilient security posture. By deploying a variety of controls at different levels of the technology stack, organizations can mitigate the risk of single points of failure and improve their overall security posture. Defense in depth includes both preventive and detective controls, such as firewalls, intrusion detection systems, and security awareness training. Access control is a critical security control that restricts and manages user access to systems, applications, and data. Effective access control ensures that only authorized individuals have access to sensitive information and resources, reducing the risk of unauthorized access and data breaches. Access control mechanisms include user authentication, authorization, and auditing. Authentication verifies the identity of users, while authorization determines what actions and resources users are permitted to access. Auditing records user activities and provides a trail of events for monitoring and investigation. To implement effective access control, organizations should adopt strong authentication methods, enforce the principle of least privilege, and regularly review and update access permissions. Encryption is another vital security control that protects data from unauthorized access or disclosure. It ensures that even if attackers gain access to encrypted data, they cannot decipher it without the appropriate decryption keys. Encryption is used to secure data at rest, in transit, and during processing. Organizations should identify and classify sensitive data, such as personally identifiable information (PII) or intellectual property, and apply encryption accordingly. Secure key management is essential for maintaining the confidentiality and integrity of encryption keys. Organizations should implement strong encryption algorithms and protocols, manage encryption keys securely, and regularly audit their encryption practices. Security patches and updates are crucial for addressing known vulnerabilities and weaknesses in software, hardware, and firmware. Software vendors and manufacturers release patches to fix security flaws and improve the overall security of their products. Organizations should establish a robust patch management process to identify, test, and deploy patches promptly. This includes prioritizing patches based on criticality and monitoring for newly released vulnerabilities. Regular patching helps prevent exploitation by attackers and reduces the attack surface.

Vulnerability management is a proactive security control that involves identifying, assessing, and remediating vulnerabilities in systems and applications. Organizations should conduct regular vulnerability scans and assessments to detect weaknesses in their environment. Once vulnerabilities are identified, they should be prioritized based on their severity and potential impact. Remediation efforts may include applying patches, implementing compensating controls, or making configuration changes. Continuous monitoring is an essential security control that involves real-time monitoring of systems, networks, and user activities. It enables organizations to detect and respond to security incidents promptly. Continuous monitoring includes activities such as log analysis, network traffic analysis, and threat intelligence feeds. Security Information and Event Management (SIEM) solutions are often used to aggregate, correlate, and analyze security data from various sources. Security incidents should be categorized, investigated, and remediated as part of the incident response process. User awareness and training play a significant role in the effectiveness of security controls. Human error and social engineering attacks are common security threats that can be mitigated through security awareness programs. Organizations should educate employees and users about security best practices, the risks of phishing and social engineering, and the importance of reporting security incidents. A well-trained workforce can serve as an additional layer of defense against security threats. Security policies and procedures provide the foundation for security controls and practices within an organization. They define the rules, responsibilities, and guidelines for implementing and maintaining security controls. Policies may cover areas such as acceptable use, data classification, incident response, and remote access. Clear and well-documented policies help ensure consistent security practices and facilitate compliance with regulatory requirements. Security controls should be implemented based on a risk assessment that considers the organization's unique threat landscape, business objectives, and regulatory requirements. A risk assessment helps identify and prioritize security controls that address the most significant risks. Security controls should align with the organization's risk tolerance and be cost-effective to implement and maintain. Organizations should also consider the potential impact of security controls on business operations and user productivity. Security controls are not static; they require regular evaluation and improvement. Organizations should conduct periodic security assessments, such as penetration testing and security audits, to identify weaknesses and areas for improvement. Lessons learned from security incidents and breaches should be used to refine security controls and incident response procedures. Compliance with regulatory requirements and industry standards often drives the implementation of specific security controls. Organizations should stay informed about relevant regulations, such as the General Data Protection Regulation (GDPR) or the Health Insurance Portability and Accountability Act (HIPAA), and ensure that their security controls align with compliance obligations. In summary, implementing effective security controls is critical for protecting information systems and data from a wide range of threats. Security controls should be selected and implemented based on the organization's risk assessment, business objectives, and regulatory requirements. A layered approach to security, including defense in depth, access control, encryption, patch management, vulnerability management, and continuous monitoring, helps create a robust security posture. Security awareness, policies, and compliance are also essential components of an effective security control framework. Regular evaluation, improvement, and alignment with industry standards and regulations are necessary to maintain strong security controls and adapt to evolving threats. In today's interconnected and digitally driven world, the threat landscape is continually evolving, and security incidents are becoming more prevalent. To effectively protect against cyber threats, organizations must not only focus on prevention but also develop robust strategies for monitoring and responding to security incidents. This chapter delves into the critical aspects of monitoring and responding to security incidents. Security incidents encompass a wide range of events that may jeopardize the confidentiality, integrity, or availability of data or systems. These events can include data breaches, malware infections, insider threats, denial-of-service attacks, and many others. Detecting and responding to security incidents promptly is essential to minimize damage and prevent further compromise. Effective incident monitoring begins with the establishment of a security operations center (SOC) or a dedicated team responsible for monitoring the organization's network and systems. The SOC is tasked with continuous monitoring, alert triage, threat detection, and incident response. To detect security incidents, organizations implement various security technologies and tools, such as intrusion detection systems (IDS), intrusion prevention systems (IPS), security information and event management (SIEM) solutions, and advanced threat detection platforms. These tools analyze network traffic, system logs, and other data sources to identify suspicious or malicious activities. Once an alert is generated, it must be triaged to determine its severity and potential impact. This involves assessing the context of the alert, reviewing relevant logs, and conducting initial investigations. The goal is to determine whether the alert represents a genuine security incident or a false positive. Intrusion detection and prevention systems play a vital role in detecting and responding to known threats. They rely on signatures and predefined rules to identify malicious patterns or activities in network traffic. However, these systems may miss previously unknown or zero-day threats. To address this limitation, organizations are increasingly adopting advanced threat detection solutions that use machine learning and behavior analysis to identify anomalous activities and potential security incidents. Effective incident response is a structured and coordinated approach to addressing security incidents when they occur. It involves a series of well-defined steps designed to contain, mitigate, and recover from the incident. One of the first steps in incident response is containment, which involves isolating the affected systems or devices to prevent further damage or compromise. This may include disabling compromised user accounts, segmenting network traffic, or taking systems offline. The goal is to limit the incident's impact and prevent it from spreading to other parts of the organization. After containment, organizations move on to the investigation phase, where they gather evidence and analyze the incident to understand its scope, impact, and root causes. This involves examining system logs, reviewing network traffic, and conducting forensic analysis. The investigation phase aims to answer critical questions, such as how the incident occurred, what data or systems were affected, and who or what was responsible. Once the investigation is complete, organizations proceed to the mitigation phase, where they take steps to remediate the vulnerabilities or weaknesses that led to the incident. This may involve applying security patches, updating configurations, or implementing additional security controls. The goal is to address the underlying issues to prevent similar incidents from occurring in the future. Communication is a critical component of incident response. Organizations should establish clear communication channels to keep stakeholders informed about the incident's progress and impact. This includes notifying senior management, legal, public relations, and regulatory authorities when required. Transparency and timely communication can help build trust with customers, partners, and employees. Legal and regulatory obligations may require organizations to report certain security incidents to authorities or affected individuals. Compliance with these requirements is essential to avoid legal repercussions and reputational damage. Incident response teams should be well-prepared and trained to handle various types of security incidents. This includes conducting tabletop exercises and simulations to test the team's response procedures and coordination. Having a well-documented incident response plan that outlines roles, responsibilities, and procedures is crucial for effective incident management. The plan should also specify the criteria for escalating incidents to senior management or law enforcement agencies, if necessary. An essential aspect of incident response is learning from past incidents. Organizations should conduct post-incident reviews to identify lessons learned and areas for improvement. This involves evaluating the effectiveness of incident response procedures, analyzing response times, and assessing the impact of incidents. The findings from these reviews should inform the organization's security posture and lead to enhancements in security controls and incident response procedures. Security incident response is not limited to technical aspects. It also includes addressing human factors, such as insider threats or social engineering attacks. Training and awareness programs should educate employees about security best practices, recognizing phishing attempts, and reporting suspicious activities. User awareness can significantly contribute to the early detection and prevention of security incidents.

In summary, monitoring and responding to security incidents are critical aspects of modern cybersecurity. Organizations must be proactive in detecting and responding to security incidents to minimize their impact and protect sensitive data and systems. Establishing a security operations center (SOC), deploying advanced threat detection solutions, and following a structured incident response process are essential components of effective incident management. By learning from past incidents and continuously improving security controls and procedures, organizations can enhance their overall security posture and resilience to evolving threats.

Chapter 10: Ethical Hacking in Practice: Real-World Scenarios

Penetration testing, often referred to as ethical hacking, is a proactive and controlled approach to assessing the security of information systems and networks. It involves simulating real-world cyberattacks to identify vulnerabilities and weaknesses that malicious actors could exploit. To conduct penetration testing effectively, security professionals follow a well-defined engagement lifecycle. This chapter explores the phases and key considerations involved in the penetration testing engagement lifecycle.

Pre-Engagement Phase: Before initiating a penetration test, there is a critical pre-engagement phase. During this phase, the penetration testing team collaborates with the client to define the scope and objectives of the test. The client and the penetration testing team establish clear goals, determine the systems and assets in scope, and agree on the rules of engagement. This phase is essential for aligning expectations, setting boundaries, and ensuring a smooth testing process.

Information Gathering Phase: The information gathering phase is the initial step of the penetration test. In this phase, the penetration testers collect as much information as possible about the target environment. This includes identifying IP addresses, domains, network ranges, and publicly available information about the organization. Open-source intelligence (OSINT) techniques and tools are commonly used to gather information.

Threat Modeling Phase: Once sufficient information is gathered, the penetration testers perform threat modeling. They analyze the collected data to identify potential threats, attack vectors, and vulnerabilities that may exist within the target environment. Threat modeling helps prioritize the areas to focus on during the test and guides the development of test scenarios.

Planning Phase: In the planning phase, the penetration testing team develops a comprehensive test plan. The plan outlines the testing methodology, techniques, and tools that will be used during the engagement. It also specifies the testing schedule, including the start and end dates of the test, as well as any specific testing windows to avoid disruption. Additionally, the plan addresses legal and compliance considerations and ensures that all necessary permissions and approvals are obtained.

Scanning and Enumeration Phase: With the plan in place, the penetration testers move on to the scanning and enumeration phase. They use scanning tools and techniques to identify active hosts, open ports, and services running on the target systems. Enumeration involves gathering detailed information about the identified services and users, such as version numbers, configurations, and user accounts.

Vulnerability Analysis Phase: In this phase, the penetration testers focus on identifying and assessing vulnerabilities. They use various vulnerability scanning tools and manual testing techniques to discover weaknesses in the target systems. Common vulnerabilities such as misconfigurations, outdated software, and known security flaws are documented and assessed for their potential impact.

Exploitation Phase: Once vulnerabilities are identified, the penetration testers move on to the exploitation phase. This is where they attempt to exploit the vulnerabilities to gain unauthorized access, escalate privileges, or compromise the target systems. It's important to note that the exploitation phase is conducted with the client's explicit consent and within the defined rules of engagement.

Post-Exploitation Phase: After successfully exploiting vulnerabilities, the penetration testers enter the post-exploitation phase. Here, they explore the compromised systems to assess the extent of the breach and gather evidence. The objective is to demonstrate the potential impact of a successful attack and identify any additional vulnerabilities that may be leveraged.

Reporting Phase: The reporting phase is a crucial aspect of penetration testing. After completing the test, the penetration testing team compiles a detailed report that includes all findings, vulnerabilities, and recommended remediation steps. The report should be clear, concise, and tailored to the technical and non-technical audience, including executives, IT teams, and security personnel.

Debriefing Phase: In the debriefing phase, the penetration testers meet with the client to discuss the findings, answer questions, and provide insights. This phase allows for open communication and knowledge *sharing between the client and the testing team. It is an opportunity to address any concerns, clarify the results, and ensure that the client fully understands the implications of the test.*

Remediation Phase: Following the penetration test, the client is responsible for addressing the identified vulnerabilities and weaknesses. The remediation phase involves implementing security patches, configuration changes, and other mitigation measures to improve the security posture. The penetration testing team may provide guidance and support during this phase to ensure that vulnerabilities are properly remediated.

Re-Engagement Phase: The penetration testing engagement lifecycle does not end with the first test. It is essential to re-engage periodically to assess the effectiveness of security improvements and identify new vulnerabilities that may arise. Re-engagements help organizations maintain a proactive approach to security and continuously enhance their defenses.

Lessons Learned Phase: After each engagement, it is essential to conduct a lessons learned session. This phase involves evaluating the overall penetration testing process, including strengths and areas for improvement. Feedback from both the client and the testing team is valuable in refining the testing methodology and approach for future engagements.

Documentation and Record Keeping: Throughout the engagement lifecycle, thorough documentation and record keeping are critical. This includes documenting the entire testing process, findings, test results, communications, and any agreed-upon actions.

Comprehensive records help maintain transparency, support compliance requirements, and provide an audit trail.

Legal and Ethical Considerations: Throughout the penetration testing engagement lifecycle, ethical and legal considerations must be upheld. Penetration testers must adhere to ethical hacking guidelines, respect the rules of engagement, and operate within the boundaries set by the client. Additionally, compliance with relevant laws and regulations, such as data protection and privacy laws, is paramount.

Continuous Improvement: The final phase of the engagement lifecycle involves continuous improvement. Organizations and penetration testing teams should continuously assess and enhance their testing methodologies, tools, and knowledge to stay ahead of evolving threats. Regular training and staying informed about the latest security trends and vulnerabilities are essential for maintaining a high level of effectiveness in penetration testing. In summary, the penetration testing engagement lifecycle is a structured and methodical approach to assessing and improving the security of information systems and networks. By following this lifecycle, organizations can proactively identify vulnerabilities, address security weaknesses, and enhance their overall cybersecurity posture. Effective penetration testing helps organizations stay ahead of potential threats and minimize the risk of cyberattacks, ultimately safeguarding critical assets and data.

Ethical hacking, also known as penetration testing or white-hat hacking, is a crucial practice in the world of *cybersecurity. It involves authorized individuals or teams simulating cyberattacks to identify vulnerabilities and weaknesses in a system, network, or application. To understand the practical application of ethical hacking, we'll explore several case studies and scenarios that showcase real-world examples of ethical hacking in action. Case Study 1: Web Application Vulnerability Assessment*

A small e-commerce business recently expanded its online presence to accommodate a growing customer base. Concerned about the security of their web application, they decided to engage an ethical hacking team to assess its vulnerabilities. The ethical hackers began by conducting a comprehensive assessment of the web application, using a combination of manual testing and automated scanning tools. During the assessment, they identified several critical vulnerabilities, including SQL injection, cross-site scripting (XSS), and insecure authentication mechanisms. The ethical hacking team provided a detailed report to the business, outlining the vulnerabilities, their potential impact, and recommended remediation steps. The business promptly addressed the vulnerabilities and implemented security measures to protect customer data. By proactively identifying and mitigating these vulnerabilities, they enhanced the security of their web application and built trust with their customers.

Case Study 2: Network Penetration Test for a Financial Institution

A financial institution with a network spanning multiple branches and data centers recognized the importance of regular security assessments. They engaged an ethical hacking team to conduct a network penetration test to evaluate the resilience of their infrastructure. The ethical hackers initiated the engagement with a comprehensive reconnaissance phase to gather information about the organization's network topology and assets. They identified potential entry points, including unpatched systems and weak access controls. Through a combination of vulnerability scanning and manual testing, the ethical hacking team successfully exploited a critical vulnerability in the organization's remote access system. This allowed them to gain unauthorized access to sensitive financial data. Upon discovery, the financial institution promptly addressed the vulnerability, reinforced its network security, and enhanced its incident response procedures. The penetration test helped the institution identify critical weaknesses and take corrective actions to prevent potential security breaches.

Case Study 3: Social Engineering and Phishing Simulation

A large multinational corporation was concerned about the increasing number of phishing attacks targeting its employees. To assess the susceptibility of their workforce to social engineering attacks, they arranged for an ethical hacking team to conduct a phishing simulation. The ethical hackers crafted convincing phishing emails that mimicked internal communications. These emails contained links to fake login pages designed to steal employee credentials. The simulated phishing campaign was executed without prior knowledge of the employees. To their surprise, a significant number of employees fell victim to the simulated phishing attacks and unknowingly provided their login credentials. Upon completion of the simulation, the ethical hacking team conducted an awareness training session for employees. They educated them on recognizing phishing attempts, the importance of strong passwords, and the significance of reporting suspicious emails. The organization also implemented email filtering and monitoring solutions to enhance its email security. Through this exercise, the corporation improved its employees' awareness and response to phishing threats, reducing the risk of successful real-world attacks.

Case Study 4: Red Team vs. Blue Team Exercise

A large government agency sought to assess the effectiveness of its cybersecurity defenses by conducting a red team vs. blue team exercise. In this scenario, the red team represented the ethical hackers attempting to infiltrate the agency's network, while the blue team comprised internal security defenders responsible for detecting and mitigating threats. The red team initiated the engagement by attempting to gain unauthorized access to the agency's network and systems. They employed various tactics, such as spear phishing, exploiting known vulnerabilities, and conducting covert reconnaissance. The blue team actively monitored the network, detected the red team's activities, and responded promptly. The exercise simulated a real-

world cyberattack scenario, allowing the blue team to test its incident response procedures and defenses. Throughout the exercise, the red team and blue team engaged in a continuous cycle of offense and defense. The red team adapted its tactics to bypass the blue team's defenses, while the blue team refined its detection and mitigation strategies. The exercise provided valuable insights into the agency's security posture, highlighting areas for improvement and helping the blue team enhance its defensive capabilities.

Case Study 5: IoT Device Vulnerability Assessment

An organization that manufactured and deployed Internet of Things (IoT) devices recognized the growing importance of IoT security. They engaged an ethical hacking team to assess the security of their IoT devices, which included smart cameras, sensors, and industrial controllers. The ethical hackers conducted a thorough assessment of the devices, analyzing their firmware, communication protocols, and access controls. They discovered multiple vulnerabilities in the devices, including default credentials, insecure firmware updates, and weak encryption. To address these vulnerabilities, the organization collaborated with the ethical hacking team to develop firmware updates and patches. They also implemented stronger access controls, secure firmware distribution mechanisms, and improved encryption protocols. By proactively addressing these IoT device vulnerabilities, the organization enhanced the security and reliability of its products, ensuring a safer and more robust IoT ecosystem.

These case studies and scenarios illustrate the practical application of ethical hacking in various domains of cybersecurity. Ethical hacking serves as a proactive approach to identifying vulnerabilities and strengthening security measures, ultimately helping organizations protect their data, systems, and reputation. By continuously assessing and improving their security posture, organizations can better defend against evolving cyber threats and maintain the trust of their stakeholders.

BOOK 2
PENTESTING 101
EXPLOITING VULNERABILITIES IN NETWORK SECURITY

ROB BOTWRIGHT

Chapter 1: Network Security Fundamentals

Network security is a fundamental aspect of modern cybersecurity, aimed at safeguarding the integrity, confidentiality, and availability of data and resources within a network. To establish a robust network security posture, it is essential to understand and apply the principles of network security effectively. Next, we will explore these principles and their significance in maintaining a secure network environment.

Defense in Depth: The principle of defense in depth emphasizes the importance of implementing multiple layers of security measures throughout a network. By having multiple layers of security, even if one layer is compromised, other layers can still provide protection. This approach includes firewalls, intrusion detection systems, access controls, and encryption.

Least Privilege: The principle of least privilege dictates that users and systems should be granted the minimum level of access or permissions required to perform their tasks. By limiting access, organizations reduce the potential for unauthorized access or misuse of resources.

Security by Design: Security should be incorporated into the design and architecture of the network from the beginning. This principle emphasizes the proactive consideration of security requirements and measures during the planning and design phases.

Continuous Monitoring: Network security is not a one-time effort but an ongoing process. Continuous monitoring involves regularly assessing the network for vulnerabilities, threats, and anomalies. It enables organizations to detect and respond to security incidents promptly.

Access Control: Access control is a critical principle that involves managing and regulating who can access specific network resources. This includes user authentication, authorization, and auditing. Access controls ensure that only authorized individuals can access sensitive information.

Patch Management: Keeping software, hardware, and firmware up to date with the latest security patches is vital. Unpatched systems are susceptible to known vulnerabilities that malicious actors can exploit. Regular patch management is essential for reducing the attack surface.

Encryption: Encryption is a fundamental technique for protecting data in transit and at rest. It ensures that even if unauthorized parties gain access to data, they cannot decipher it without the appropriate decryption keys. Encryption is used for securing communications, data storage, and sensitive information.

Auditing and Logging: Auditing and logging activities on the network provide a record of events and actions. These logs are valuable for monitoring, forensic analysis, and compliance with regulatory requirements.

Incident Response: Having a well-defined incident response plan is crucial. It outlines the actions to be taken in the event of a security incident. An effective incident response plan helps minimize the impact of security breaches and facilitates recovery.

User Education and Awareness: Users are often the weakest link in network security. Educating and raising awareness among users about security best practices, threats, and social engineering tactics is essential. An informed workforce can recognize and report security incidents.

Segmentation: Network segmentation involves dividing a network into smaller, isolated segments. Each segment has its security controls and access policies. Segmentation limits lateral movement for attackers and reduces the potential blast radius of a breach.

Redundancy and High Availability: Ensuring redundancy and high availability of critical network components and resources is essential for minimizing downtime and ensuring business continuity. Redundant systems and failover mechanisms can prevent service disruptions.

Authentication and Authorization: Authentication verifies the identity of users or systems trying to access network resources, while authorization determines what actions and resources they are allowed to use. Strong authentication methods and proper authorization are crucial for controlling access.

Firewalls and Intrusion Detection Systems (IDS): Firewalls and IDS play a vital role in network security. Firewalls filter incoming and outgoing traffic based on predefined rules, while IDS monitor network traffic for suspicious activity. Both help prevent unauthorized access and detect potential threats.

Regular Security Assessments: Conducting regular security assessments, such as vulnerability scans and penetration tests, helps identify weaknesses and vulnerabilities within the network. These assessments are essential for ongoing improvement.

Data Classification: Data should be classified based on its sensitivity and importance. Classified data can then be protected according to its classification level, with stricter controls for highly sensitive information.

Secure Configuration Management: Properly configuring network devices and systems is critical. Misconfigurations can introduce security vulnerabilities. Establishing and maintaining secure configuration baselines is essential.

Zero Trust: The Zero Trust model assumes that no one, whether inside or outside the network, can be trusted by default. Access is only granted based on continuous authentication and verification. By implementing these principles of network security, organizations can establish a strong defense against a wide range of threats and vulnerabilities. Network security is an ongoing effort that requires vigilance and adaptation to evolving threats and technologies. By incorporating these principles into their network security strategies, organizations can enhance their overall security posture and protect their valuable assets and data.

Networks are the backbone of modern businesses and organizations, facilitating communication, data sharing, and collaboration. However, this interconnectedness also makes them susceptible to a wide range of security threats. Understanding these common network security threats is essential for organizations to develop effective defenses and protect their assets.

Malware: Malware, short for malicious software, includes viruses, worms, Trojans, spyware, and ransomware. Malware is designed to infiltrate systems and disrupt operations, steal sensitive information, or hold data hostage for ransom.

Phishing: Phishing is a deceptive tactic used by cybercriminals to trick individuals into revealing sensitive information, such as usernames, passwords, or credit card details. Phishing attacks often involve convincing emails or websites that appear legitimate.

Distributed Denial of Service (DDoS) Attacks: DDoS attacks involve overwhelming a network or website with an excessive amount of traffic, causing it to become unavailable to users. Attackers use botnets or other means to orchestrate these attacks.

Insider Threats: Insider threats come from individuals within an organization who misuse their access and privileges. These individuals may have malicious intent or unknowingly compromise security through negligence.

Man-in-the-Middle (MitM) Attacks: MitM attacks occur when an attacker intercepts communication between two parties. The attacker can eavesdrop on the conversation or modify the data being transmitted, leading to potential data theft or unauthorized access.

Zero-Day Exploits: Zero-day exploits target vulnerabilities in software or hardware that are not yet known to the vendor. Attackers exploit these vulnerabilities before a patch or fix is available, making them difficult to defend against.

Password Attacks: Password attacks involve attempting to guess or crack passwords to gain unauthorized access to accounts or systems. Techniques include brute force attacks, dictionary attacks, and credential stuffing.

SQL Injection: SQL injection attacks target web applications that use improperly sanitized user inputs. Attackers inject malicious SQL queries into input fields, potentially gaining access to a database and sensitive data.

Cross-Site Scripting (XSS): XSS attacks occur when attackers inject malicious scripts into webpages viewed by other users. These scripts can steal information or perform actions on behalf of the victim without their consent.

Social Engineering: Social engineering attacks manipulate individuals into divulging sensitive information or taking specific actions. Common techniques include pretexting, baiting, and tailgating.

Eavesdropping: Eavesdropping involves intercepting and monitoring network traffic to obtain confidential information. Attackers may use packet sniffers or other methods to capture data.

Credential Theft: Credential theft can occur through various means, such as keyloggers, phishing, or data breaches. Attackers steal usernames and passwords, potentially gaining access to multiple accounts.

Malvertising: Malvertising involves malicious advertisements that distribute malware when clicked or viewed. These ads can appear on legitimate websites and compromise user devices.

IoT Vulnerabilities: Internet of Things (IoT) devices often have weak security, making them vulnerable to attacks. Attackers may compromise IoT devices to gain access to networks or launch DDoS attacks.

Data Theft: Data theft encompasses the unauthorized access or theft of sensitive data, including intellectual property, customer information, and financial records. Attackers may sell stolen data on the dark web or use it for extortion.

Ransomware: Ransomware encrypts a victim's data and demands a ransom for the decryption key. Successful ransomware attacks can result in data loss and financial consequences.

Drive-By Downloads: Drive-by downloads occur when malware is automatically downloaded and installed on a user's device without their consent. This can happen when visiting compromised websites or clicking on malicious links.

Brute Force Attacks: Brute force attacks involve systematically attempting all possible combinations of passwords or keys to gain access to a system or account. These attacks are time-consuming but can be successful if weak passwords are used.

Software Vulnerabilities: Exploiting vulnerabilities in software or operating systems is a common tactic. Attackers search for and exploit security flaws to gain access or execute malicious code.

Email-based Attacks: Beyond phishing, email-based attacks include email spoofing, where attackers manipulate email headers to appear as if the email is from a legitimate source. These attacks can be used for various purposes, including spreading malware or deceiving recipients.

Malicious Insider Actions: In addition to inadvertent insider threats, some individuals within organizations may intentionally engage in malicious activities, such as stealing sensitive data, for personal gain or harm.

Fileless Malware: Fileless malware operates in memory, leaving no traces on the file system. This makes it difficult to detect and remove, as traditional antivirus solutions may not identify it.

Supply Chain Attacks: Supply chain attacks target vulnerabilities in the supply chain ecosystem. Attackers *compromise trusted suppliers or vendors to infiltrate target organizations.*

Advanced Persistent Threats (APTs): APTs are sophisticated, long-term attacks conducted by well-funded and organized threat actors. They aim to remain undetected while infiltrating networks and exfiltrating data.

Data Interception: Data interception involves intercepting and capturing data as it travels between devices or across networks. Attackers use this technique to steal sensitive information, such as login credentials or financial data.

Understanding these common network security threats is crucial for organizations and individuals alike. By recognizing the various methods employed by malicious actors, security measures can be implemented to mitigate risks and protect against potential cyberattacks. Vigilance, security awareness, and proactive defenses are essential in today's interconnected digital landscape.

Chapter 2: Scanning and Enumeration of Network Devices

Network scanning is a fundamental component of network security assessments, providing valuable insights into the state of a network, its devices, and potential vulnerabilities. These techniques enable security professionals to identify weaknesses, misconfigurations, and areas of concern within a network. Next, we delve into various network scanning techniques, their purposes, and considerations for their use. Network scanning is the systematic process of exploring a network to discover active hosts, open ports, and services running on those hosts. Scanning serves as a reconnaissance phase in both offensive and defensive security assessments. The primary objectives of network scanning are to gather information about the network's structure, identify potential entry points, and detect vulnerabilities. One of the most common and basic network scanning techniques is the use of ping sweeps and port scans. Ping sweeps involve sending Internet Control Message Protocol (ICMP) echo requests to a range of IP addresses to determine which hosts are online. Port scans, on the other hand, involve probing a host's ports to identify which ones are open and listening for connections. Ping sweeps and port scans help security professionals create a map of the network and identify potential targets for further assessment. Another essential network scanning technique is the banner grabbing or banner enumeration. Banner grabbing involves connecting to open ports on a target host and gathering information from the banners or service banners. These banners typically contain details about the service or application running on the port, including its version number and sometimes even the operating system. Banner grabbing helps security professionals identify specific services and their versions, aiding in vulnerability assessment and targeting. While these basic techniques are valuable for initial reconnaissance, more advanced scanning methods are available for in-depth analysis. One such technique is the use of network scanning tools, such as Nmap (Network Mapper). Nmap is a versatile and widely used open-source tool that can perform a wide range of network scans. It can identify hosts, open ports, services, and even attempt to determine the underlying operating system. Nmap supports various scanning techniques, including SYN scans, TCP connect scans, and UDP scans. SYN scans are stealthy and efficient, while TCP connect scans are more accurate but less stealthy. UDP scans are used to identify services running over UDP, which is connectionless and less predictable than TCP. Besides Nmap, there are other network scanning tools available, each with its strengths and capabilities. Wireshark, for instance, is a packet analysis tool that can capture and analyze network traffic, helping security professionals identify vulnerabilities and anomalies. Masscan is another tool known for its speed in conducting massive scans across large IP address ranges. When performing network scans, ethical considerations and legal constraints must be followed. Scanning networks without proper authorization can lead to legal repercussions, as it can be seen as an intrusive and potentially harmful activity. Security professionals should always obtain explicit permission from network owners or administrators before conducting any form of scanning. Additionally, during network scans, it is crucial to minimize disruption to network operations. Scanning can generate significant traffic, potentially causing performance issues or even denial of service (DoS) conditions on target hosts. Therefore, security professionals should carefully choose scanning parameters, such as scan intensity and timing, to avoid disrupting network operations. Beyond standard scanning techniques, specialized scans can be employed to target specific vulnerabilities or gain deeper insights. Vulnerability scans, for example, focus on identifying known vulnerabilities within network services and applications. These scans use databases of known vulnerabilities and attempt to match them with the services and versions detected during the scan. Vulnerability scans provide security professionals with a prioritized list of weaknesses that require remediation. Another specialized scanning technique is the use of credentialed scans. Credentialed scans involve providing valid login credentials to target hosts, allowing the scanner to gather more detailed information and assess configurations accurately. These scans are particularly useful for identifying misconfigurations and vulnerabilities that may not be visible to external scans. While network scanning is a valuable tool for security professionals, it is essential to use it responsibly and *ethically. Unauthorized or aggressive scanning can disrupt network operations, violate privacy, and potentially lead to legal consequences. Security professionals should always obtain proper authorization and follow best practices when conducting network scans. In summary, network scanning is a crucial aspect of network security assessments. It provides insights into the network's structure, identifies potential vulnerabilities, and aids in the development of robust security measures. Security professionals should leverage a variety of scanning techniques and tools while adhering to ethical and legal considerations to maintain the integrity and security of the networks they assess. Network enumeration is a critical phase in the process of understanding and assessing a network's security. It involves the systematic discovery and documentation of open ports and services on target hosts. Understanding what ports are open and what services are running is essential for network administrators and security professionals. This chapter explores the importance of port and service enumeration and the techniques and tools used for this purpose. When you're tasked with securing a network or performing a security assessment, knowing which ports are open and what services are running on those ports is vital. Ports are like doors or gateways on a networked device, and services are the applications or processes that use these ports to communicate. Each open port represents a potential entry point into a system, and each service running on that port may have its security vulnerabilities. By enumerating open ports and services, you gain valuable insights into the network's structure and potential attack vectors. One of the most straightforward methods of port enumeration is using the "netstat" command. Netstat (short for network statistics) is a command-line tool available on most operating systems, including Windows, Linux, and macOS. Typing "netstat -an" will display a list of all active network connections and their associated ports. This provides a snapshot of the current network state, showing which ports are in use and the addresses they are connected to. While netstat is useful for quickly checking open ports on a local system, it has limitations when scanning remote systems or an entire network. For more comprehensive port and service enumeration, network scanning tools like Nmap come into play. Nmap, or Network Mapper, is a powerful open-source tool designed for network discovery and security auditing. It allows you to scan large networks, identify open ports and services, and even attempt to determine the underlying operating system. Nmap provides various scanning techniques, such as SYN scans, TCP connect scans, and UDP scans. A SYN scan is stealthy and efficient, while a TCP connect scan is more accurate but less stealthy. UDP scans are used to identify services running over UDP, which is connectionless and less predictable than TCP. When using Nmap for port enumeration, you can specify a range of IP addresses to scan and a range of ports to target. For example, "nmap -p 1-1000 192.168.1.0/24" scans the IP range 192.168.1.0 to 192.168.1.255 for ports 1 to 1000. Nmap will provide a list of open ports and their associated* services on each target host. Beyond Nmap, there are other tools available for port and service enumeration, each with its strengths and capabilities. One such tool is Masscan, known for its speed in conducting massive scans across large IP address ranges. Masscan is particularly useful when you need to scan a large network quickly. While scanning for open ports is essential, identifying the services running on those ports is equally important. Service enumeration involves determining the type and version of the service running on an open port. This information helps security professionals assess potential vulnerabilities and weaknesses. Nmap, in addition to identifying open ports, can also attempt to determine the service and its version using various techniques, including banner grabbing. Banner grabbing involves connecting to an open port and gathering information from the service banner or response. Service banners typically contain details about the service or application running on the port, such as its version number. While Nmap provides valuable information about open ports and services, it is essential to use it responsibly and ethically. Scanning networks without proper authorization can lead to legal repercussions, as it can be seen as intrusive and potentially harmful. Security professionals should always obtain explicit permission from network owners or administrators before conducting any form of scanning. Additionally, during port and service enumeration, it is crucial to minimize disruption to network operations. Scanning can generate significant traffic, potentially causing performance issues or even *denial of service (DoS) conditions on target hosts. Therefore, security professionals should carefully choose scanning parameters, such as scan intensity and timing, to avoid disrupting network operations. In summary, enumerating open ports and services is a fundamental step in network security assessments. It provides critical information about the network's structure, potential vulnerabilities, and attack vectors. Security professionals should leverage tools like Nmap, Masscan, and others while adhering to ethical and legal considerations. By understanding and documenting open ports and services, organizations can develop robust security measures and protect against potential cyber threats.*

Chapter 3: Exploiting Weaknesses in Network Protocols

Network protocols are essential for communication between devices and systems in a network, but they can also introduce security vulnerabilities. Understanding these vulnerabilities is crucial for securing a network effectively. This chapter explores some common network protocols and the vulnerabilities associated with them. Network protocols serve as the rules and conventions that devices follow to communicate over a network. They dictate how data is formatted, transmitted, and received, enabling devices to understand and interact with each other. While these protocols are essential for network functionality, they can become points of weakness if not properly secured. Let's explore some of the vulnerabilities commonly found in network protocols.

Transmission Control Protocol (TCP):

TCP is a fundamental protocol for reliable data transmission, but it is vulnerable to TCP/IP stack fingerprinting, which can be used to identify the operating system of a host.

TCP is also susceptible to SYN flooding attacks, where an attacker overwhelms a target system with connection requests, causing resource exhaustion.

Another TCP vulnerability is session hijacking, where an attacker intercepts and takes control of an established session, potentially gaining unauthorized access.

Internet Protocol (IP):

IP is the backbone of the internet, but its lack of built-in security mechanisms makes it vulnerable to IP spoofing, where attackers manipulate the source IP address of packets to impersonate trusted sources.

Another vulnerability in IP is the routing information protocol (RIP) vulnerability, which can be exploited for route injection and unauthorized access.

Simple Network Management Protocol (SNMP):

SNMP is used for network management, but its default community strings (essentially passwords) are often left unchanged, making it vulnerable to unauthorized access.

Weak SNMP configurations can lead to information disclosure and network control by attackers.

Domain Name System (DNS):

DNS translates domain names into IP addresses, but it can be vulnerable to DNS cache poisoning, where attackers manipulate DNS caches to redirect traffic to malicious destinations.

DNS tunneling is another concern, allowing attackers to exfiltrate data covertly through DNS requests and responses.

Hypertext Transfer Protocol (HTTP):

HTTP is the foundation of the World Wide Web, but it is vulnerable to various attacks, including cross-site scripting (XSS), where malicious scripts are injected into webpages viewed by other users.

SQL injection is another HTTP vulnerability, enabling attackers to execute malicious SQL queries through web application inputs.

File Transfer Protocol (FTP):

FTP is used for transferring files, but it can expose sensitive data due to plain text transmission of credentials, making it susceptible to eavesdropping.

Additionally, FTP bounce attacks can allow attackers to use an FTP server as a proxy to scan other hosts.

Secure Shell (SSH):

SSH is widely used for secure remote access, but it can be vulnerable to brute force attacks if weak or default passwords are in use.

Weak SSH configurations may also allow unauthorized access to critical systems.

Border Gateway Protocol (BGP):

BGP is essential for internet routing, but it can be vulnerable to BGP hijacking, where attackers divert internet traffic to their own networks.

Incorrect BGP configurations can lead to traffic interception and manipulation.

Dynamic Host Configuration Protocol (DHCP):

DHCP is used for automatic IP address assignment, but it can be vulnerable to DHCP spoofing attacks, where rogue DHCP servers provide malicious configuration to clients.

Unauthorized DHCP servers can disrupt network operations and potentially route traffic through malicious hosts.

Post Office Protocol (POP) and Internet Message Access Protocol (IMAP):

POP and IMAP are used for email retrieval, but they can be susceptible to unauthorized access if weak authentication methods are used.

Cleartext transmission of credentials in some configurations can expose sensitive email content.

Simple Mail Transfer Protocol (SMTP):

SMTP is used for sending email, but it can be vulnerable to email spoofing, enabling attackers to send messages impersonating trusted sources.

Open relay SMTP servers can also be abused for spam email distribution.

Network Time Protocol (NTP):

NTP is used for time synchronization, but it can be vulnerable to NTP amplification attacks, where attackers exploit misconfigured NTP servers to amplify their traffic, facilitating DDoS attacks.

Weak NTP configurations can lead to inaccurate timekeeping and synchronization issues.

Session Initiation Protocol (SIP):

SIP is used for VoIP communication, but it can be vulnerable to SIP scanning and enumeration, allowing attackers to identify and potentially exploit SIP devices.

Weak SIP configurations can lead to unauthorized call interception and eavesdropping.

Extensible Messaging and Presence Protocol (XMPP):

XMPP is used for instant messaging and presence information, but it can be vulnerable to XMPP spam, where attackers flood XMPP servers with unsolicited messages.

Weak XMPP configurations can lead to message interception and impersonation.

File Transfer Protocol Secure (FTPS):

FTPS is a secure version of FTP, but misconfigurations can lead to vulnerabilities, such as weak encryption or improper certificate validation.

FTPS vulnerabilities can expose sensitive data during file transfers.

Virtual Private Network (VPN) Protocols:

VPN protocols like PPTP and L2TP can be vulnerable to brute force attacks if weak authentication methods or pre-shared keys are used.

Insecure VPN configurations can lead to unauthorized access to private networks. It is essential to recognize that vulnerabilities in network protocols are not limited to the ones mentioned here. Network security requires continuous monitoring, updates, and adherence to best practices to mitigate these vulnerabilities effectively. By understanding the weaknesses in common network protocols, organizations can implement appropriate security measures to protect their networks and data.

Network protocols are the foundation of communication in modern computer networks, enabling devices and systems to interact seamlessly. However, these protocols can contain vulnerabilities and weaknesses that, when exploited, can lead to unauthorized access and potentially compromise the security of the network. Next, we delve into the techniques and strategies used by malicious actors to exploit protocol weaknesses and gain unauthorized access. Understanding these methods is crucial for network administrators and security professionals to develop effective defenses. Protocol weaknesses can manifest in various forms, from implementation flaws to design flaws. Malicious actors *often exploit these weaknesses to compromise the confidentiality, integrity, or availability of network resources. One common protocol weakness that attackers target is weak authentication mechanisms. Authentication is the process of verifying the identity of a user or device before granting access. Weak authentication can allow attackers to bypass login or access controls, posing a significant security risk. For example, many legacy protocols use cleartext passwords, which are vulnerable to eavesdropping and interception. Attackers can intercept login credentials and use them for unauthorized access. Additionally, weak password policies, such as default or easily guessable passwords, can also lead to unauthorized access. Malicious actors frequently attempt to exploit these weaknesses through techniques like password guessing and brute force attacks. Another protocol weakness that attackers exploit is insufficient encryption or encryption-related vulnerabilities. Encryption is essential for protecting the confidentiality and integrity of data in transit. When encryption is weak or improperly configured, attackers can intercept and manipulate data. For instance, the Transport Layer Security (TLS) protocol, which secures web communications, can be vulnerable to downgrade attacks. Attackers can force the use of weaker encryption algorithms, making it easier to decrypt and manipulate data. Furthermore, some protocols may use outdated or insecure encryption algorithms, making them susceptible to cryptographic attacks. Weak encryption can result in data leakage and unauthorized access to sensitive information. Additionally, attackers may target protocols with inadequate access controls or improper session management. Access controls determine who can access specific resources or perform certain actions within a network. When access controls are weak or misconfigured, attackers can gain unauthorized access to restricted areas. For example, an attacker may manipulate URL parameters in a web application to access administrative features intended for privileged users. Likewise, improper session management can lead to unauthorized access. If a web application fails to destroy session cookies after logout, an attacker could use a stolen session cookie to impersonate a legitimate user. Session fixation attacks are another concern, where attackers set a user's session identifier to a known value, enabling them to hijack the session. Furthermore, protocol weaknesses can manifest in the form of design flaws that attackers exploit. One such weakness is the lack of adequate input validation and output encoding. Input validation ensures that data entered by users is safe and does not contain malicious code. Lack of input validation can allow attackers to inject malicious payloads, such as SQL injection or cross-site scripting (XSS) attacks. These attacks can lead to unauthorized access, data leakage, or even complete system compromise. Similarly, insufficient output encoding can enable attackers to inject malicious content into the responses sent by a server. Attackers may manipulate web forms, injecting JavaScript code that runs in the context of other users' browsers, leading to session theft or other malicious* actions. Moreover, attackers often target insecure deserialization in protocols. Serialization is the process of converting data into a format suitable for storage or transmission. Deserialization is the reverse process, where data is reconstructed from its serialized form. Insecure deserialization vulnerabilities can allow attackers to execute arbitrary code during the deserialization process. For example, an attacker could manipulate serialized objects to execute malicious code on a server, potentially gaining unauthorized access or causing other security breaches. Furthermore, some protocols may lack proper error handling mechanisms. Error handling is essential for gracefully dealing with unexpected situations or input. When protocols do not handle errors effectively, attackers can exploit these situations to gain unauthorized access. For example, a poorly designed authentication protocol may provide verbose error messages that disclose whether a username exists. Attackers can use this information to enumerate valid usernames and focus their efforts on brute force attacks. Beyond these weaknesses, attackers may exploit specific protocol vulnerabilities, such as buffer overflows or protocol-specific flaws. Buffer overflows occur when a program writes data beyond the boundaries of a buffer, potentially allowing attackers to execute arbitrary code. Attackers may send specially crafted packets to a vulnerable protocol implementation, triggering a buffer overflow and compromising the system. Protocol-specific vulnerabilities can also lead to unauthorized access. For example, a vulnerability in the Server Message Block

(SMB) protocol, commonly used for file sharing in Windows networks, could allow remote code execution or unauthorized access to shared resources. In summary, exploiting protocol weaknesses for unauthorized access is a significant concern in network security. Malicious actors continuously search for vulnerabilities in network protocols, seeking opportunities to compromise security. Network administrators and security professionals must remain vigilant, implementing robust security measures, conducting regular audits, and staying informed about emerging threats. By addressing protocol weaknesses and implementing strong security practices, organizations can reduce the risk of unauthorized access and protect their networks from potential security breaches.

Chapter 4: Gaining Unauthorized Access to Network Resources

In the world of cybersecurity, password cracking and brute-force attacks represent two fundamental techniques employed by attackers to gain unauthorized access to systems and accounts. Understanding these methods is essential for both security professionals and individuals to strengthen their defenses against such threats. Password cracking involves the process of attempting to uncover a user's password by various means, typically through systematic guessing or decryption. Attackers use a variety of techniques and tools to crack passwords, exploiting vulnerabilities in password security. One of the most straightforward methods employed in password cracking is dictionary attacks. Dictionary attacks involve trying every word from a predefined list, often compiled from common words, phrases, or combinations of characters. Attackers use these lists to systematically test each possibility until they find the correct password. This method is effective against weak and commonly used passwords but is less likely to succeed against complex or unique ones. To increase their chances of success, attackers may augment dictionary attacks with variations, such as adding numbers, symbols, or common substitutions (e.g., replacing "o" with "0" or "e" with "3"). Another common password cracking technique is brute-force attacks. Brute-force attacks are straightforward and exhaustive, systematically testing all possible combinations of characters until the correct password is found. This method is highly effective but can be extremely time-consuming and resource-intensive, especially for longer and more complex passwords. Brute-force attacks can target both character-based passwords (alphanumeric) and passphrases (a sequence of words or a sentence). For character-based passwords, attackers start with single-character combinations and progressively increase the length of the tested strings until the correct password is discovered. For passphrases, attackers test various combinations of words, spaces, and characters to uncover the passphrase. While brute-force attacks are powerful, they are also resource-intensive and time-consuming, making them less practical for longer and complex passwords. To mitigate the effectiveness of brute-force attacks, organizations and individuals should enforce strong password policies that include requirements for length, complexity, and regular password changes. Additionally, multi-factor authentication (MFA) provides an extra layer of security, requiring users to provide additional authentication factors beyond just a password. These factors can include something the user knows (password), something the user has (a smartphone or token), or something the user is (biometrics like fingerprints or facial recognition). MFA significantly enhances security by making it much more difficult for attackers to gain unauthorized access, even if they manage to crack a password. Beyond dictionary and brute-force attacks, attackers may employ more sophisticated techniques like rainbow table attacks. Rainbow tables are precomputed tables of hash values for commonly used passwords or character combinations. When an attacker gains access to a hashed password, they can compare it against the values in the rainbow table to find a matching plaintext password. This method is faster than brute-force attacks but requires significant storage for the rainbow tables. Defending against rainbow table attacks involves using strong and unique salts (random values added to passwords before hashing) for each user. Salts make it impractical for attackers to use precomputed tables effectively. In addition to these techniques, attackers may leverage password spraying attacks. Password spraying attacks involve trying a few common passwords against a large number of accounts. This approach aims to avoid account lockouts and detection while still having a chance of success. Attackers may target multiple accounts with the same commonly used passwords, hoping that at least one of them will have weak credentials. To protect against password spraying attacks, organizations should implement account lockout policies that temporarily lock accounts after a certain number of failed login attempts. Additionally, monitoring for unusual login patterns and enforcing strong password policies can deter attackers. Another advanced technique used in password cracking is the use of specialized hardware, such as graphics processing units (GPUs) and field-programmable gate arrays (FPGAs). These hardware accelerators can perform large numbers of hash calculations in parallel, significantly speeding up the *password cracking process. To counter this, organizations should consider employing key derivation functions (KDFs) that introduce computational delays during password hashing, making it more difficult and time-consuming for attackers to crack passwords using specialized hardware. It's crucial for individuals and organizations to recognize the importance of strong, unique passwords. Weak passwords are the primary target for attackers, as they provide the easiest path to unauthorized access. A strong password should be lengthy, contain a mix of uppercase and lowercase letters, numbers, and special characters, and avoid common words or phrases. Password managers can assist users in generating and storing complex passwords securely. Educating users about the significance of strong passwords and regular password changes is also essential in maintaining a robust security posture. In summary, password cracking and brute-force attacks remain prevalent threats in the world of cybersecurity. Attackers continuously evolve their techniques to compromise user credentials and gain unauthorized access to systems and accounts. Understanding these threats and implementing strong security measures, such as strong password policies, multi-factor authentication, account lockout policies, and key derivation functions, is crucial for defending against password-related attacks. By taking these precautions, individuals and organizations can significantly enhance their security and protect against unauthorized access. Privilege escalation is a critical concept in cybersecurity, involving the process of gaining higher levels of access and control over a system or network than what is initially authorized. Understanding the methods and techniques used by attackers for privilege escalation is vital for security professionals to defend against such threats effectively. Unauthorized access methods often serve as the first step towards privilege escalation. Attackers seek to breach systems, networks, or applications to gain initial access. Common methods for unauthorized access include exploiting vulnerabilities, using stolen credentials, or leveraging social engineering. One prevalent method is exploiting software vulnerabilities, often in operating systems or applications. Attackers search for weaknesses in software and use them to gain entry. This may involve exploiting buffer overflows, injecting malicious code, or finding unpatched vulnerabilities. Once inside, attackers can move laterally and escalate their privileges to gain further control. Another method is the use of stolen or brute-forced credentials. Attackers acquire login information through various means, such as password cracking, phishing attacks, or credential theft. With valid credentials, attackers can gain access to systems and potentially escalate their privileges. Social engineering is another approach where attackers manipulate individuals into revealing sensitive information, like passwords or access credentials. This method relies on psychological manipulation and deception. Phishing, pretexting, and baiting are common techniques used in social engineering. Once attackers have achieved unauthorized access, the next step is privilege escalation. They seek to acquire higher levels of control and access rights, often surpassing their initial permissions. One common method for privilege escalation is exploiting misconfigured or vulnerable software components. Attackers search for weaknesses in system configurations, service settings, or access controls. For example, they may discover a service running with elevated privileges that can be exploited. By leveraging these vulnerabilities, attackers can gain higher access levels. Another technique is privilege escalation through kernel exploits. Attackers target vulnerabilities in the operating system's kernel, which is the core component responsible for managing system resources. Exploiting these vulnerabilities allows attackers to execute code at the highest privilege level, often referred to as "kernel mode." Privilege escalation through kernel exploits provides full control over the system and is a highly sought-after goal for attackers. Kernel vulnerabilities are particularly valuable to attackers because they provide a pathway to complete system compromise. Moreover, attackers may attempt privilege escalation through the abuse of misconfigured permissions and access control lists (ACLs). This method involves exploiting errors in permission settings to gain unauthorized access. For example, an attacker may identify a directory with overly permissive permissions, allowing them to read, write, or execute files they shouldn't have access to. Privilege escalation through misconfigured permissions can occur on both the file system and within applications. Attackers also exploit known privilege escalation vulnerabilities in software and operating systems. These are vulnerabilities that are publicly documented and can be leveraged to escalate privileges. Attackers scan systems for unpatched software or services that contain these vulnerabilities. By exploiting them, they can gain higher levels of access. Moreover, privilege escalation may involve "token manipulation." Tokens are data structures used by the operating system to represent a user's identity and privileges. Attackers may manipulate these tokens to impersonate other users or acquire elevated privileges. Token manipulation techniques include "token stealing" and "token impersonation." Additionally, attackers may employ "DLL hijacking" or "DLL planting" to escalate privileges. Dynamic Link Libraries (DLLs) are shared code libraries used by many Windows applications. By placing a malicious DLL in a directory that is searched by an application, attackers can execute arbitrary code within the context of that application, potentially gaining higher privileges. Another avenue for privilege escalation is "password cracking." If attackers have access to password hashes or encrypted credentials, they can attempt to crack the passwords to gain access to privileged accounts. Tools like John the Ripper or Hashcat are commonly used for this purpose. Attackers may also exploit vulnerabilities in authentication mechanisms. For instance, they may identify flaws in single sign-on (SSO) implementations or multi-factor authentication (MFA) systems. By circumventing these mechanisms, attackers can access privileged accounts without proper authentication. In summary, privilege escalation is a significant concern in cybersecurity, as attackers continuously seek ways to gain higher levels of access and control within systems and networks. Understanding the methods and techniques employed by attackers is essential for security professionals to develop effective defense strategies. Implementing strong access controls, regularly patching and updating software, monitoring for unusual activities, and educating users about security best practices are crucial steps in preventing unauthorized access and privilege escalation. By taking these precautions, individuals and organizations can enhance their security posture and protect against these threats effectively.*

Chapter 5: Sniffing and Intercepting Network Traffic

Packet sniffing is a fundamental and powerful technique in the field of network security and analysis. It involves capturing and inspecting data packets as they traverse a network, providing valuable insights into network activity. However, the same technique can also be exploited by malicious actors for nefarious purposes. Next, we will explore packet sniffing techniques, their uses in both legitimate and unauthorized contexts, and strategies for mitigating the associated risks. Packet sniffing, also known as network sniffing or packet analysis, is the process of intercepting and examining data packets as they pass through a network. These packets contain information such as source and destination IP addresses, port numbers, protocols, and the actual data being transmitted. Packet sniffing tools, also known as network analyzers or packet capture tools, are essential for this task. They capture packets from the network interface, store them for analysis, and provide detailed insights into network traffic. Legitimate uses of packet sniffing include network troubleshooting, performance monitoring, and security analysis. Network administrators and security professionals rely on packet sniffing to diagnose network issues, optimize network performance, and identify security threats. For example, when troubleshooting network problems, packet sniffing can reveal the source of network congestion, dropped packets, or communication errors. In security analysis, it is used to detect suspicious activities, such as unauthorized access attempts or malware communication. On the other hand, unauthorized packet sniffing can pose significant security risks. Malicious actors may employ packet sniffing to eavesdrop on network traffic and gather sensitive information, such as login credentials, personal data, or confidential business information. To mitigate the risks associated with packet sniffing, it is crucial to understand the techniques used in both legitimate and unauthorized contexts. Promiscuous mode is a fundamental aspect of packet sniffing. Network interfaces, by default, only capture packets destined for their own MAC address or broadcast traffic. In promiscuous mode, an interface captures all packets on the network segment, regardless of their destination. This mode is essential for effective packet sniffing, as it allows the capture of traffic not specifically addressed to the sniffing device. Packet sniffing can be done using both software-based and hardware-based methods. Software-based packet sniffing utilizes software tools installed on a computer or network device. These tools interact with the network interface to capture and analyze packets. Wireshark is a popular example of a software-based packet sniffing tool. Hardware-based packet sniffing, on the other hand, relies on dedicated hardware appliances designed for packet capture and analysis. These appliances are often used in high-speed networks and data centers where the volume of traffic makes software-based solutions impractical. They offer specialized hardware capabilities for efficient packet processing and analysis. Packet sniffing can also be categorized into passive and active sniffing. Passive sniffing involves capturing network packets without actively sending packets or generating traffic. This method is stealthier and less likely to be detected by network intrusion detection systems. Active sniffing, on the other hand, involves sending packets onto the network to provoke responses from other devices. This method can be more intrusive and may increase the risk of detection. Packet sniffing techniques can be classified into three main categories: hub-based sniffing, switch-based sniffing, and router-based sniffing. Hub-based sniffing involves connecting the sniffing device to a network hub, which broadcasts all incoming packets to all connected devices. While hubs are relatively simple and inexpensive, they are becoming less common in modern networks, as they are less efficient than switches. Switch-based sniffing is the most common method, as it allows for more targeted packet capture. Switches forward packets only to the devices that need them, preventing unnecessary packet distribution. To perform switch-based sniffing, attackers may employ techniques like ARP spoofing or MAC flooding to trick the switch into broadcasting packets to the sniffing device. Router-based sniffing involves placing the sniffing device between two routers or in a position where it can capture traffic passing through. This method can be complex and may require physical access to the network infrastructure. To mitigate the risks associated with packet sniffing, organizations should implement encryption mechanisms, such as SSL/TLS for web traffic and VPNs for remote access. Encryption protects the confidentiality of data even if it is intercepted by packet sniffers. Additionally, network segmentation and access controls help limit the exposure of sensitive information to potential sniffers. Regular monitoring of network traffic and anomaly detection can help identify unauthorized sniffing activities. It is essential to keep software and *hardware up to date with the latest security patches to prevent attackers from exploiting known vulnerabilities for packet sniffing. Moreover, strong authentication and access controls on network devices can prevent unauthorized individuals from gaining physical access to the network infrastructure. In summary, packet sniffing is a powerful technique with both legitimate and unauthorized uses. Understanding the methods employed by malicious actors is essential for organizations to protect their networks and sensitive information. Implementing encryption, access controls, network monitoring, and regular updates are crucial steps in mitigating the risks associated with packet sniffing. By taking these precautions, organizations can maintain the confidentiality and integrity of their network traffic, even in the face of potential sniffing attempts. Once network traffic has been captured using packet sniffing techniques, the next crucial step is to analyze the captured data thoroughly. Effective analysis provides valuable insights into network behavior, security threats, and performance issues. Next, we will explore the process of analyzing captured network traffic, the tools and techniques used, and how this analysis can benefit network administrators and security professionals. The analysis of captured network traffic is a vital aspect of network monitoring, troubleshooting, and security. By examining the packets that traverse a network, administrators can gain a deep understanding of network activity, identify potential issues, and detect security threats. One fundamental tool for network traffic analysis is Wireshark, a popular open-source packet analyzer. Wireshark allows users to load captured packet data and provides a user-friendly* interface for exploring and dissecting network traffic. The first step in analyzing captured traffic is to open the capture file in a packet analyzer like Wireshark. The capture file contains the recorded packets, and the analyzer presents this data in a structured and readable format. Once the capture file is loaded, users can start examining the packets. It's essential to set specific goals for the analysis to ensure that the process is focused and efficient. For instance, the analysis may aim to troubleshoot slow network performance, detect suspicious activity, or investigate an incident. One common use of network traffic analysis is to diagnose network performance issues. When users report slow or unreliable network connectivity, administrators can analyze captured traffic to pinpoint the source of the problem. By examining packet timing, errors, and retransmissions, they can identify bottlenecks, congestion, or network misconfigurations. Moreover, network traffic analysis can reveal patterns of usage and bandwidth consumption. Administrators can identify which applications or services are consuming the most bandwidth and address any congestion issues. Security professionals also rely on network traffic analysis to detect and investigate security incidents. When analyzing captured traffic for security purposes, the focus is on identifying anomalous or suspicious behavior. This may include unusual traffic patterns, unrecognized devices on the network, or communication with known malicious IP addresses. The goal is to identify potential security threats, such as malware infections, data exfiltration attempts, or unauthorized access. To aid in the detection of security threats, packet analyzers like Wireshark offer features like *packet filtering and custom alerts. Filters allow users to narrow down the analysis to specific types of traffic or protocols, making it easier to spot irregularities. Custom alerts can be set up to trigger notifications when specific conditions or patterns are detected, providing real-time alerts for potential threats. Another critical aspect of network traffic analysis is protocol analysis. Network protocols define how data is structured, transmitted, and processed on the network. Analyzing the behavior of different protocols can help administrators understand network interactions, diagnose issues, and identify potential vulnerabilities. For example, analyzing the behavior of the HTTP protocol can reveal web application vulnerabilities, such as SQL injection or cross-site scripting (XSS) attacks. Similarly, analysis of the Domain Name System (DNS) protocol can uncover suspicious domain lookups, which may indicate malware activity or command and control communications. Additionally, network traffic analysis can help with incident response. When a security incident occurs, analysts can review captured traffic to understand the scope and impact of the incident. They can identify the initial point of compromise, track lateral movement within the network, and determine what data or systems may have been compromised. This information is crucial for developing a response plan and implementing remediation measures. In some cases, analysts may use historical network traffic data for forensic analysis. This involves examining past network traffic to reconstruct events, identify the root cause of incidents, and gather evidence for legal or investigative purposes. Captured traffic data can serve as a valuable source of evidence in digital forensics investigations. To make the most of* captured network traffic data, it's essential to have a solid understanding of network protocols and their behavior. This knowledge helps analysts interpret the data accurately and identify unusual or suspicious patterns. Moreover, keeping up-to-date with emerging threats and attack techniques is crucial for effective network traffic analysis. Attackers continually evolve their methods, so analysts must adapt their analysis techniques accordingly. In summary, analyzing captured network traffic is a critical skill for network administrators and security professionals. It provides valuable insights into network performance, security threats, and incident response. By using tools like Wireshark and employing protocol analysis, filtering, and custom alerts, professionals can gain a deep understanding of their network's behavior and detect potential issues or security threats. Network traffic analysis plays a vital role in maintaining the reliability and security of modern computer networks.

Chapter 6: Denial of Service (DoS) Attacks and Mitigation

In the realm of cybersecurity, Denial-of-Service (DoS) and Distributed Denial-of-Service (DDoS) attacks represent some of the most prevalent and disruptive threats that organizations face today. These attacks are designed to overwhelm a target system or network, rendering it inaccessible to legitimate users. Next, we will delve into the concepts, techniques, motivations, and countermeasures associated with DoS and DDoS attacks. DoS attacks are a category of cyberattacks that focus on disrupting the availability of a target system or network. They achieve this disruption by overwhelming the target with a flood of traffic or resource requests, thereby exhausting its capacity to respond to legitimate users. DoS attacks can target various resources, including web servers, network infrastructure, or even individual user accounts. One common type of DoS attack is the "flood attack," where the attacker sends an excessive volume of traffic to the target, consuming its network bandwidth or server resources. Another form of DoS attack is the "logic attack," which exploits vulnerabilities in the target's software or application logic to consume CPU or memory resources until the system becomes unresponsive. Attackers may also employ "resource depletion attacks," such as exhausting connection pools, memory, or available file descriptors. These attacks exploit weaknesses in resource management to disrupt the target's normal operation. DoS attacks can have severe consequences, ranging from website downtime and loss of revenue to reputational damage and customer dissatisfaction. While DoS attacks involve a single source of attack traffic, DDoS attacks take the threat to a whole new level by involving multiple sources. A DDoS attack harnesses a network of compromised computers, often referred to as a botnet, to launch a coordinated assault on the target. The sheer volume of traffic generated by a botnet can easily overwhelm even well-prepared targets. The distributed nature of DDoS attacks makes them more challenging to defend against compared to DoS attacks. Motivations for launching DoS and DDoS attacks vary, including financial gain, revenge, competitive advantage, hacktivism, and ideological reasons. Some attackers launch these attacks to extort money from victims by demanding a ransom to cease the attack. Others may use DoS and DDoS attacks as a form of protest or retaliation. Competitors may seek to gain an edge in the marketplace by disrupting a rival's online services. Hacktivists use these attacks to advance their ideological or political agendas, while some individuals simply engage in them for the thrill of causing disruption. To defend against DoS and DDoS attacks, organizations must implement a multi-layered security strategy that encompasses various aspects of network, application, and infrastructure security. One fundamental defense is network traffic filtering and rate limiting. By filtering out malicious traffic at the network perimeter and imposing rate limits, organizations can reduce the impact of DoS and DDoS attacks. Web application firewalls (WAFs) can also help protect against application-layer DoS attacks by inspecting and filtering traffic at the application level. In addition to these measures, organizations should consider deploying intrusion detection and prevention systems (IDPS) to detect and block suspicious traffic patterns associated with DoS and DDoS attacks. Anomaly-based detection systems can identify unusual traffic patterns and trigger alerts or countermeasures. Furthermore, content delivery networks (CDNs) can distribute traffic across multiple geographically dispersed servers, helping to absorb and mitigate the impact of DDoS attacks. CDNs also provide services like traffic scrubbing, which filters out malicious traffic before it reaches the target's infrastructure. To counter DDoS attacks, organizations can implement rate limiting, traffic profiling, and traffic rerouting strategies. Rate limiting restricts the volume of requests accepted from a single source or IP address, reducing the impact of flood attacks. Traffic profiling analyzes incoming traffic to identify patterns associated with DDoS attacks and applies countermeasures accordingly. Traffic rerouting involves diverting attack traffic away from the target infrastructure to a separate mitigation infrastructure, where the malicious traffic can be filtered and discarded. Moreover, organizations should create an incident response plan specifically tailored to address DoS and DDoS attacks. This plan should outline procedures for detecting, mitigating, and recovering from attacks, as well as identifying responsible parties and coordinating with law enforcement, if necessary. Regular testing and simulation of DoS and DDoS attack scenarios can help organizations refine their response procedures and improve their resilience. In summary, DoS and DDoS attacks remain significant threats in the cybersecurity landscape, capable of causing severe disruption and financial losses to organizations. Understanding the motivations, techniques, and countermeasures associated with these attacks is essential for effective defense. By implementing a combination of network filtering, rate limiting, traffic profiling, CDN services, and a robust incident response plan, organizations can reduce their vulnerability and mitigate the impact of DoS and DDoS attacks. Proactive measures and preparedness are key to maintaining the availability and integrity of online services in the face of these persistent threats.

In the ever-evolving landscape of cybersecurity, the mitigation and prevention of Denial-of-Service (DoS) incidents are of paramount importance for organizations seeking to protect their networks, services, and data from disruptive attacks. A successful DoS attack can lead to downtime, financial losses, and damage to an organization's reputation, making it imperative to have a robust strategy in place. Next, we will explore various techniques and best practices for mitigating and preventing DoS incidents effectively. Mitigating and preventing DoS incidents require a multifaceted approach that encompasses both proactive measures and reactive responses. One of the fundamental strategies for DoS mitigation is network traffic filtering. By implementing ingress and egress traffic filtering at the network perimeter, organizations can block or limit the volume of malicious traffic attempting to reach their infrastructure. This filtering can be based on various criteria, such as source IP addresses, traffic patterns, or known attack signatures. Ingress filtering prevents traffic with spoofed or illegitimate source IP addresses from entering the network, a common tactic used in DoS attacks. Egress filtering, on the other hand, restricts the traffic leaving the network, preventing malicious traffic from being launched from within. Rate limiting is another effective technique for mitigating DoS attacks, especially those involving flood-based attacks. By limiting the rate at which incoming traffic is accepted, organizations can reduce the impact of high-volume attacks, such as UDP reflection and amplification attacks. Traffic shaping is a related approach that involves prioritizing and controlling the flow of network traffic to ensure the availability of essential services during an attack. Web Application Firewalls (WAFs) play a crucial role in protecting web services from application-layer DoS attacks. WAFs inspect incoming traffic at the application level and filter out malicious requests and payloads. They can identify and block excessive or malicious requests, safeguarding web applications from overloading or being exploited. Content Delivery Networks (CDNs) are valuable assets for mitigating and preventing DoS incidents. CDNs distribute incoming traffic across multiple geographically dispersed servers, reducing the impact of volumetric attacks by absorbing and distributing the load. Furthermore, CDNs offer traffic scrubbing services that filter out malicious traffic before it reaches the target's infrastructure. Another approach to DoS mitigation involves rate limiting, traffic profiling, and traffic rerouting. Rate limiting restricts the volume of requests accepted from a single source, reducing the impact of flood attacks. Traffic profiling analyzes incoming traffic to identify patterns associated with DoS attacks and applies countermeasures accordingly. Traffic rerouting diverts attack traffic away from the target infrastructure to a separate mitigation infrastructure, where the malicious traffic can be filtered and discarded. Proactive measures to prevent DoS incidents include capacity planning and redundancy. Organizations should assess their network and server capacity to ensure they can handle traffic spikes and increased loads during an attack. Redundancy in critical infrastructure components, such as load balancers and servers, can also help maintain service availability in the event of a DoS attack. Implementing intrusion detection and prevention systems (IDPS) can aid in the early detection and mitigation of DoS attacks. Anomaly-based detection systems can identify unusual traffic patterns and trigger alerts or countermeasures. Additionally, regular patch management and software updates are essential to prevent attackers from exploiting known vulnerabilities for DoS attacks. Unpatched or outdated software can serve as a vector for launching attacks or amplifying their impact. Security Information and Event Management (SIEM) solutions provide real-time monitoring and alerting capabilities that help organizations detect and respond to DoS incidents promptly. These systems can aggregate and analyze logs and alerts from various sources, providing a holistic view of network activity. Organizations should also develop an incident response plan specifically tailored to address DoS incidents. This plan should outline procedures for detecting, mitigating, and recovering from attacks, as well as identifying responsible parties and coordinating with law enforcement, if necessary. Regular testing and simulation of DoS attack scenarios can help organizations refine their response procedures and improve their resilience. Moreover, organizations can consider the use of traffic management and load balancing solutions to distribute incoming traffic across multiple servers or data *centers. This approach enhances the overall availability and performance of online services while providing a level of redundancy against DoS attacks. Furthermore, the use of intrusion prevention systems (IPS) can help organizations automatically block or mitigate known attack patterns, reducing the manual intervention required during an attack. Educating employees and end-users about security best practices, such as recognizing and reporting suspicious activities, can help prevent DoS attacks that originate from within the organization. In summary, mitigating and preventing DoS incidents require a comprehensive and proactive approach. Organizations must employ a combination of network traffic filtering, rate limiting, traffic profiling, traffic rerouting, and intrusion detection and prevention systems. These measures should be complemented by capacity planning, redundancy, patch management, incident response planning, and security awareness training. By implementing a robust defense strategy and staying vigilant, organizations can reduce their vulnerability to DoS attacks and ensure the availability and integrity of their online services.*

Chapter 7: Intrusion Detection and Prevention Systems

In the ever-evolving landscape of cybersecurity, the implementation of Intrusion Detection Systems (IDS) and Intrusion Prevention Systems (IPS) has become crucial for organizations seeking to safeguard their networks, systems, and data. These security solutions play a pivotal role in detecting and responding to unauthorized and malicious activities. Next, we will explore the concepts, deployment strategies, and best practices associated with IDS and IPS solutions. An Intrusion Detection System (IDS) is a security mechanism designed to monitor network and system activities and identify suspicious or potentially harmful behavior. It operates by inspecting traffic patterns, event logs, and other data sources to detect signs of unauthorized access, security policy violations, or known attack patterns. An IDS operates in two primary modes: signature-based and anomaly-based. In signature-based detection, the IDS compares observed activities with a predefined set of attack signatures or patterns. When a match is found, the IDS generates an alert or takes predefined actions to mitigate the threat. This method is effective at identifying known attack patterns but may miss novel or zero-day attacks. Anomaly-based detection, on the other hand, establishes a baseline of normal network and system behavior. The IDS then continuously monitors activities and generates alerts when deviations from the baseline occur. While this approach can detect previously unknown threats, it may also generate false positives if legitimate activities appear anomalous. Intrusion Prevention Systems (IPS), on the other hand, not only detect but also actively block or mitigate threats in real-time. They function similarly to IDS but have the capability to take automated actions to prevent or contain attacks. IPS solutions can be configured to drop malicious packets, block IP addresses, or implement rate limiting to thwart attack attempts. One of the key challenges in implementing IDS and IPS solutions is choosing the appropriate deployment model. There are three primary deployment models: network-based, host-based, and hybrid. Network-based IDS and IPS solutions are positioned within the network infrastructure to monitor traffic passing through them. They analyze network packets, making them well-suited for detecting and mitigating network-level threats, such as port scans, malware communications, and suspicious traffic patterns. Host-based IDS and IPS solutions, on the other hand, are installed on individual host systems. They monitor and analyze activities at the host level, including log files, system calls, and file integrity. This deployment model is effective at detecting threats that may not traverse the network, such as local privilege escalation or malicious software installation. Hybrid solutions combine elements of both network-based and host-based deployments. They offer a comprehensive view of network and host activities and are suitable for organizations seeking a balance between the two approaches. Another crucial consideration in implementing IDS and IPS solutions is fine-tuning and *customizing the detection rules and policies. Signature-based detection relies on up-to-date attack signatures and patterns, so organizations should regularly update their rule sets to protect against emerging threats. Anomaly-based detection requires careful tuning to establish an accurate baseline of normal behavior and reduce false positives. Organizations should define policies for how the IDS and IPS solutions should respond to detected threats. These policies may include actions such as generating alerts, blocking traffic, or quarantining compromised systems. The response strategy should align with the organization's risk tolerance and incident response plan. Additionally, organizations should integrate IDS and IPS solutions into their overall security architecture. This includes coordinating with other security tools, such as firewalls, antivirus software, and Security Information and Event Management (SIEM) systems. By sharing information and collaborating, these tools can enhance the overall security posture and provide a holistic view of the threat landscape. Regular monitoring and analysis of IDS and IPS alerts are essential to detect and respond to security incidents effectively. Security teams should investigate and prioritize alerts based on severity and potential impact. Incident response procedures should be well-documented and regularly tested to ensure a rapid and effective response to detected threats. Continuous monitoring and analysis of network and system logs can help organizations identify patterns and trends that may indicate ongoing attacks or emerging threats. Additionally, organizations should conduct regular* vulnerability assessments and penetration tests to identify potential weaknesses that may be exploited by attackers. By proactively addressing vulnerabilities, organizations can reduce the likelihood of successful intrusions. In summary, implementing IDS and IPS solutions is a critical component of a robust cybersecurity strategy. These systems provide the capability to detect, prevent, and respond to a wide range of threats, from known attack patterns to novel threats and zero-day vulnerabilities. The choice of deployment model, fine-tuning of detection rules and policies, and integration with other security tools are essential factors for success. Regular monitoring, analysis, and incident response planning round out the approach, ensuring that organizations can effectively protect their networks, systems, and data from evolving threats. In the ever-evolving landscape of cybersecurity, intrusion alerts serve as a crucial early warning system, providing organizations with the means to detect and respond to potential security incidents promptly. When an intrusion alert is generated, it signifies that an event or activity within the network or system has triggered a security sensor or monitoring tool. Next, we will explore the concepts, strategies, and best practices associated with analyzing and responding to intrusion alerts effectively. The process of analyzing and responding to intrusion alerts is an essential aspect of cybersecurity incident detection and response. It involves assessing the significance of the alert, investigating the event or activity that triggered it, and determining whether it represents a genuine security incident. The goal is to *identify and mitigate security threats, prevent further unauthorized access, and minimize the impact on the organization's systems and data. The first step in analyzing an intrusion alert is to review the alert details provided by the security sensor or monitoring tool. These details typically include information about the nature of the alert, the affected system or resource, the timestamp of the event, and relevant context or metadata. Understanding the alert's specifics is crucial for determining the severity and potential impact of the incident. Intrusion alerts are often categorized by severity levels, ranging from informational or low impact to critical or high impact. The severity level helps security analysts prioritize their response efforts and allocate resources accordingly. Once the alert details have been reviewed, the next step is to investigate the event or activity that triggered the alert. This investigation may involve examining log files, network traffic captures, system configurations, and other relevant data sources. The goal is to gain a deeper understanding of the event's context, scope, and potential implications. Security analysts should also consider the alert's source and credibility. Is the alert generated by a trusted and well-configured security sensor or monitoring tool, or could it be a false positive? False positives occur when security sensors incorrectly interpret normal or benign activities as security threats. Analysts should assess whether the alert aligns with known attack patterns, threat intelligence, or indicators of compromise (IOCs). IOCs are pieces of information that indicate potential malicious activity, such as IP* addresses, domain names, file hashes, or malware signatures. Comparing the alert data to IOCs can help determine whether the event is consistent with known threats. During the investigation, security analysts may use various tools and techniques to gather additional information and corroborate their findings. These tools may include network packet analyzers, log analysis tools, endpoint security solutions, and forensic analysis software. Analyzing network traffic patterns, system logs, and system memory dumps can provide valuable insights into the nature of the intrusion and its impact on the affected systems. In some cases, analysts may need to perform memory or disk forensics to recover additional evidence. Once the investigation is complete, security analysts should assess whether the intrusion alert represents a genuine security incident or a false positive. This determination is crucial for deciding on the appropriate response actions. False positives should be documented and used to improve the accuracy of intrusion detection systems. If the alert is confirmed as a legitimate security incident, the next step is to assess the incident's severity and potential impact. This assessment considers factors such as the compromised systems, the type of data involved, the attacker's capabilities, and the attack's duration and persistence. Incident severity helps organizations prioritize their response efforts and allocate resources effectively. After assessing the incident's severity and impact, security analysts should formulate a response plan. This plan outlines the actions and steps required to contain, mitigate, and recover from the security incident.

Response actions may include isolating compromised systems from the network, implementing security patches, changing passwords, and restoring affected systems from backups. In cases where sensitive data has been exposed, organizations may need to notify affected individuals or regulatory authorities, as required by data protection laws and regulations. Throughout the incident response process, effective communication and coordination among security teams, IT personnel, management, and external stakeholders are critical. Clear and timely communication ensures that response efforts are well-coordinated, and key decision-makers are informed. In addition to responding to the immediate security incident, organizations should conduct a post-incident analysis or debriefing. This analysis involves reviewing the incident response process, identifying areas for improvement, and updating security policies and procedures based on lessons learned. The goal is to enhance the organization's resilience and preparedness for future security incidents. Regularly testing and simulating intrusion alert scenarios through red teaming or penetration testing exercises can help organizations evaluate their detection and response capabilities. In summary, analyzing and responding to intrusion alerts are essential components of effective cybersecurity incident detection and response. Security analysts must assess the alert's severity, investigate the triggering event, corroborate findings with relevant data sources, and determine whether the alert represents a genuine security incident. If an incident is confirmed, a well-

defined response plan should be executed to contain, mitigate, and recover from the security breach. Effective communication and coordination among stakeholders are critical for successful incident response. Regular post-incident analysis and testing help organizations continuously improve their incident response capabilities and overall security posture. By following best practices and staying vigilant, organizations can detect and respond to security incidents promptly, minimizing their impact and protecting their systems and data.

Chapter 8: Wireless Network Vulnerabilities and Attacks

In the modern world, Wi-Fi has become an integral part of our daily lives, enabling us to connect our devices to the internet without the constraints of wired connections. However, the convenience of Wi-Fi also comes with security challenges and vulnerabilities that can be exploited by malicious actors. Next, we will explore the various weaknesses and threats associated with Wi-Fi networks, and discuss strategies to mitigate these risks. Wi-Fi networks are susceptible to a range of security weaknesses, with one of the most common being weak or default passwords. Many Wi-Fi routers come with default usernames and passwords that are often unchanged by users, making them easy targets for attackers. Additionally, the use of easily guessable passwords or the absence of strong authentication measures can leave Wi-Fi networks vulnerable to unauthorized access. Another common weakness in Wi-Fi security is the use of outdated encryption protocols. WEP (Wired Equivalent Privacy), for example, was once widely used but is now considered highly insecure, as it can be easily cracked by determined attackers. Even WPA (Wi-Fi Protected Access) and WPA2, once considered secure, have been found to have vulnerabilities that can be exploited by attackers. The emergence of the WPA3 standard has improved security, but many older devices and routers still use less secure encryption methods. Open Wi-Fi networks, those that do not require a password to connect, are convenient but come with significant security risks. Attackers can easily connect to open Wi-Fi networks and intercept traffic, potentially capturing sensitive information. Guest networks, commonly used to provide internet access to visitors, can also pose security risks if not properly isolated from the main network. Rogue access points, unauthorized Wi-Fi devices that mimic legitimate networks, can be used by attackers to trick users into connecting to them. Once connected, attackers can intercept and manipulate network traffic, potentially leading to data breaches. Wi-Fi networks are vulnerable to various forms of eavesdropping and packet sniffing attacks. Attackers can use tools and techniques to capture data packets transmitted over the airwaves, potentially gaining access to sensitive information, such as login credentials or confidential documents. Even encrypted Wi-Fi networks can be susceptible to these attacks if encryption keys are compromised. Wi-Fi networks can be targeted by various denial-of-service (DoS) attacks that disrupt network operations and connectivity. Attackers can flood a network with traffic or use deauthentication attacks to disconnect legitimate users from the network. These attacks can lead to service disruptions, network outages, and loss of productivity. Wi-Fi networks in public places, such as coffee shops, airports, and hotels, are often targeted by attackers seeking to exploit unsuspecting users. These attackers may set up rogue Wi-Fi hotspots with enticing names, luring users to connect to them. Once connected, attackers can intercept data, steal login credentials, or deliver malware to connected devices. The practice of war driving, where individuals drive around searching for vulnerable Wi-Fi networks, is another threat to Wi-Fi security. Attackers equipped with Wi-Fi scanning tools can identify open or poorly secured networks and potentially gain unauthorized access. To mitigate Wi-Fi security weaknesses and vulnerabilities, organizations and individuals can implement several best practices. First and foremost, it is essential to change default usernames and passwords on Wi-Fi routers and access points. Use strong, unique passwords that are difficult to guess, and consider enabling two-factor authentication for added security. Regularly update the firmware of Wi-Fi devices to ensure that known security vulnerabilities are patched. Use strong encryption protocols, such as WPA3, to protect Wi-Fi traffic, and avoid using outdated and insecure encryption methods. Segment Wi-Fi networks by creating separate guest networks that are isolated from the main network. This helps prevent unauthorized access to sensitive data and devices. Implement strong access controls by limiting the number of devices that can connect to the Wi-Fi network and using MAC address filtering to only allow trusted devices. Consider using a virtual private network (VPN) when connecting to public Wi-Fi networks to encrypt data traffic and protect sensitive information. When connecting to public Wi-Fi, avoid connecting to open networks and be cautious when selecting networks with similar names to known hotspots. Use a trusted VPN service to encrypt your internet traffic and protect your data from potential eavesdropping. Regularly monitor Wi-Fi networks for unauthorized devices and unusual activity, which can be indicative of a security breach. Employ intrusion detection and prevention systems (IDS/IPS) to detect and respond to suspicious network activity. In summary, Wi-Fi networks are susceptible to a range of security weaknesses and vulnerabilities that can be exploited by attackers. These weaknesses include weak passwords, outdated encryption protocols, open networks, rogue access points, eavesdropping, DoS attacks, and more. To mitigate these risks, organizations and individuals should follow best practices such as changing default passwords, using strong encryption, segmenting networks, implementing access controls, and using VPNs when connecting to public Wi-Fi. By taking these steps, Wi-Fi users can enhance the security of their networks and protect sensitive information from potential threats. In the realm of cybersecurity, wireless networks have become ubiquitous, providing connectivity and convenience in various environments. However, their widespread use also makes them attractive targets for attackers looking to exploit vulnerabilities and gain unauthorized access. Next, we will delve into the various techniques employed by attackers to exploit wireless networks and discuss strategies for securing them against these threats. One of the most common wireless network exploitation techniques is the use of weak or default passwords. Many individuals and organizations fail to change the default login credentials on their wireless routers and access points. Attackers can easily exploit this oversight by attempting to log in with default usernames and passwords, gaining unauthorized access to the network. Another prevalent technique is the use of brute-force attacks to crack Wi-Fi passwords. Attackers employ automated tools that systematically try different combinations of passwords until they discover the correct one. This method can be successful if the password is weak or easily guessable. Encryption weaknesses in Wi-Fi protocols are also exploited by attackers. For example, vulnerabilities in older encryption standards like WEP (Wired Equivalent Privacy) and WPA (Wi-Fi Protected Access) have been leveraged to compromise networks. Additionally, attackers may attempt to capture Wi-Fi handshake packets and use offline attacks to crack the encryption key. Rogue access points are another common method used to exploit wireless networks. Attackers set up unauthorized access points with names similar to legitimate networks, tricking users into connecting to them. Once connected, attackers can intercept data, steal credentials, or launch further attacks. Eavesdropping attacks involve the interception of wireless communications. Attackers use tools to capture and monitor data packets transmitted over the airwaves. This allows them to potentially intercept sensitive information, such as login credentials or confidential data. Denial-of-service (DoS) attacks can disrupt wireless networks by flooding them with traffic, rendering them unusable. Attackers may also launch deauthentication attacks, disconnecting legitimate users from the network. These attacks can lead to service *disruptions and network outages. Evil twin attacks involve the creation of a malicious access point that mimics a legitimate network. Users unknowingly connect to the evil twin, allowing attackers to intercept data and potentially launch further attacks. Attackers can exploit vulnerabilities in wireless router firmware and access point software to gain unauthorized access. Unpatched or outdated firmware may contain security flaws that attackers can exploit to compromise the network. To secure wireless networks against these exploitation techniques, organizations and individuals can implement several best practices. First and foremost, it is crucial to change default usernames and passwords on wireless routers and access points. Use strong, unique passwords that are resistant to brute-force attacks. Regularly update the firmware of wireless devices to patch known vulnerabilities and ensure they are protected against exploitation. Use strong encryption protocols like WPA3 to protect wireless traffic from eavesdropping. Disable older and less secure encryption methods like WEP. Implement strong access controls by limiting the number of devices that can connect to the network and using MAC address filtering to only allow trusted devices. Regularly monitor wireless networks for rogue access points and unusual activity, which may indicate a security breach. Employ intrusion detection and prevention systems (IDS/IPS) to detect and respond to suspicious wireless network activity. Segment wireless networks from the main network to isolate potential threats. Implement wireless intrusion detection systems (WIDS) to actively monitor and detect unauthorized access and attacks on the wireless network. Educate users about the risks of connecting to open or unsecured Wi-Fi networks and the importance of using VPNs when connecting to public Wi-Fi. In summary, wireless networks are vulnerable to a range of exploitation techniques that attackers can use to gain unauthorized access, intercept data, and disrupt services. These techniques include weak passwords, brute-force attacks, encryption vulnerabilities, rogue access points, eavesdropping, denial-of-service attacks, evil twin attacks, and exploiting software vulnerabilities. To protect wireless networks, organizations and individuals should follow best practices such as changing default credentials, updating firmware, using strong encryption, implementing access controls, monitoring for rogue access points, and educating users about security risks. By taking these steps, wireless network users can enhance their security posture and safeguard their data and communications from potential threats.*

Chapter 9: Securing Network Infrastructure

In the ever-evolving landscape of cybersecurity, network hardening stands as a fundamental practice for organizations seeking to secure their digital assets and protect against a wide range of threats. Network hardening involves implementing a series of security measures and best practices to reduce vulnerabilities and fortify the network's defenses. Next, we will explore these best practices and strategies for effectively hardening your network. One of the foundational steps in network hardening is keeping all network devices and software up to date. Regularly applying security patches and updates ensures that known vulnerabilities are addressed promptly, reducing the risk of exploitation by attackers. This applies not only to operating systems but also to routers, switches, firewalls, and all network infrastructure components. Implementing strong access controls is essential for network security. This includes using strong, unique passwords for all devices and regularly changing them. Consider implementing multi-factor authentication (MFA) for added protection, requiring users to provide multiple forms of identification before granting access. Segmenting the network into separate zones with distinct security policies is another key practice. By isolating critical assets from less sensitive areas, you can limit the potential impact of a security breach. Firewalls play a crucial role in network hardening, acting as gatekeepers that filter incoming and outgoing traffic. Configuring firewalls to allow only necessary traffic and blocking unnecessary or risky connections helps reduce the attack surface.

Implementing intrusion detection and prevention systems (IDS/IPS) can further enhance network security. These systems monitor network traffic for suspicious activity and can automatically block or alert on potential threats. Encryption is a powerful tool for protecting data in transit. Using secure protocols like HTTPS for web traffic and VPNs for remote access helps ensure that sensitive information remains confidential. Regularly auditing network configurations is essential for identifying and addressing security weaknesses. Conducting security assessments and penetration testing can help uncover vulnerabilities before attackers can exploit them. Keeping an inventory of all authorized devices and services on the network helps detect unauthorized or rogue components. Implementing network monitoring and logging is critical for identifying and responding to security incidents. Monitoring tools can detect unusual activity, while logs provide a record of network events for analysis and forensic purposes. Network administrators should follow the principle of least privilege when granting access to network resources. Users and devices should only have the permissions necessary to perform their specific tasks, reducing the risk of unauthorized access. Implementing strong physical security measures is often overlooked but crucial. Ensure that network equipment is physically protected from tampering or theft, and restrict physical access to data centers and network closets. Implementing proper data backup and disaster recovery plans is essential for network resilience. Regularly backing up critical data and systems ensures that, in the event of a security incident or hardware failure, data can be restored promptly. Network administrators should regularly review and update security *policies and procedures to adapt to evolving threats. Educating employees and users about security best practices and conducting security awareness training helps create a security-conscious culture. Implementing remote access controls and secure authentication methods is vital for safeguarding the network from unauthorized access by remote users. Virtual private networks (VPNs) and secure remote desktop protocols add layers of security to remote access. Regularly conducting security assessments and vulnerability scanning helps identify weaknesses that need to be addressed. Implementing network access controls and network segmentation can limit the reach of attackers if they breach one part of the network. Intrusion detection and prevention systems should be configured to actively monitor and respond to threats in real-time. Implementing secure configurations and best practices for network devices and software is essential. This includes disabling unnecessary services, removing default accounts and passwords, and following vendor-recommended security guidelines. Regularly monitoring network traffic and analyzing logs can help detect and respond to security incidents promptly. Implementing incident response plans and procedures ensures that the organization is prepared to address security breaches effectively. Regularly updating and patching all network components is crucial for addressing known vulnerabilities. Conducting regular security assessments and penetration tests helps uncover potential weaknesses. Monitoring network traffic and analyzing logs can provide insights into suspicious or malicious activities. Implementing strong access controls and user authentication methods is vital for preventing unauthorized access. Segmenting the network and implementing firewalls can help limit the attack surface. Educating employees and users about security best practices and the importance of cybersecurity awareness creates a security-conscious culture. In summary, network hardening is a critical practice for organizations seeking to secure their digital assets and protect against a wide range of cyber threats. It involves implementing a series of security measures and best practices, including patch management, strong access controls, network segmentation, firewalls, intrusion detection and prevention systems, encryption, and regular security assessments. By following these best practices and continually adapting to evolving threats, organizations can enhance their network security and reduce the risk of cyberattacks and data breaches. In the ever-changing landscape of cybersecurity, organizations face an array of threats and challenges that require a proactive and strategic approach to safeguarding their digital assets and sensitive information. Implementing security controls and policies is a fundamental aspect of an organization's overall cybersecurity strategy. These controls and policies are designed to establish a framework for protecting information, managing risks, and ensuring compliance with relevant regulations. Next, we will delve into the importance of implementing security controls and policies, the key components involved, and strategies for effective implementation. Security controls are measures, safeguards, or countermeasures that organizations put in place to protect their information systems and data. They are essential for identifying and mitigating risks, preventing security breaches, and responding to incidents. Security policies, on the other hand, are documented* guidelines and rules that define an organization's approach to cybersecurity. They outline expectations, responsibilities, and procedures related to information security. One of the primary objectives of implementing security controls and policies is to reduce the organization's exposure to threats and vulnerabilities. This reduction of risk helps protect sensitive data, maintain business continuity, and preserve the organization's reputation. Security controls and policies are also crucial for ensuring compliance with industry-specific regulations and data protection laws. These regulations often require organizations to implement specific security measures and demonstrate their commitment to safeguarding customer data and privacy. Implementing security controls and policies involves several key components and considerations. First and foremost, organizations must conduct a thorough risk assessment to identify potential threats, vulnerabilities, and the potential impact of security incidents. This assessment serves as the foundation for designing and implementing appropriate controls and policies. Based on the risk assessment, organizations should define their security objectives and goals. These objectives help guide the selection and implementation of security controls and policies that align with the organization's overall strategy. Selecting the right security controls and policies is crucial. These may include technical measures such as firewalls, antivirus software, and encryption, as well as administrative measures such as access controls, incident response plans, and employee training. The chosen controls and policies should be tailored to the organization's specific needs and risk profile. Once the controls and policies are selected, *organizations must establish clear roles and responsibilities. This includes designating individuals or teams responsible for implementing, managing, and monitoring the controls and policies. Communication and awareness play a vital role in the successful implementation of security controls and policies. Organizations should educate employees and stakeholders about the importance of cybersecurity, their roles in safeguarding information, and the specific policies and procedures they need to follow. Regular training and awareness programs help reinforce these principles and ensure that everyone understands their role in the organization's security efforts. The implementation of security controls and policies should be an ongoing and iterative process. Organizations should regularly assess the effectiveness of their controls and policies, update them as needed, and adapt to evolving threats and technologies. Continuous monitoring of security measures is essential for identifying and responding to security incidents promptly. Incident response plans and procedures should be well-defined and tested regularly to ensure a rapid and effective response to security breaches. Documentation is a critical aspect of implementing security controls and policies. Organizations should maintain detailed records of their security measures, policies, procedures, and incidents. This documentation serves as a valuable resource for auditing, compliance reporting, and incident analysis. Regular audits and assessments should be conducted to evaluate the effectiveness of security controls and policies. These assessments can help identify weaknesses and areas for improvement. Compliance with industry-specific regulations and data protection laws should be a top priority. Organizations must stay informed about the latest regulatory requirements and ensure that their security controls and policies align with these standards. In summary, implementing security controls and policies is a fundamental aspect of an organization's cybersecurity strategy. These controls and policies are essential for reducing risk, protecting sensitive data, ensuring compliance, and responding effectively to security incidents. To successfully implement security controls and policies, organizations must conduct a thorough risk assessment, define clear objectives, select appropriate measures, establish roles and responsibilities, communicate and educate employees, and maintain an ongoing commitment to monitoring and improvement. By following these best practices, organizations can enhance their cybersecurity posture and better protect their digital assets and sensitive information.*

Chapter 10: Advanced Network Penetration Testing Techniques

In the realm of cybersecurity, understanding the network landscape and identifying potential vulnerabilities are critical components of any comprehensive security strategy. Port scanning and enumeration are essential techniques that cybersecurity professionals use to gather information about target systems and networks. These techniques provide valuable insights into the network's structure, services, and potential security weaknesses. Next, we will explore advanced port scanning and enumeration techniques, their importance, and strategies for effective utilization. Port scanning is the process of probing a target system or network to discover open ports and services. Open ports are like doors that allow data to flow in and out of a system, and they are crucial for the functionality of various network services and applications. However, open ports can also be avenues for attackers to exploit vulnerabilities and gain unauthorized access. Enumeration, on the other hand, is the process of extracting additional information about the target system, such as user accounts, shares, and system configurations, once open ports have been identified. Effective port scanning and enumeration play a pivotal role in vulnerability assessment, penetration testing, and securing network infrastructure. One of the most common and straightforward port scanning techniques is TCP connect scanning. In this method, the scanner attempts to establish a full TCP connection with each target port to determine if it is open. While effective, this approach can be slow and easily detected by intrusion detection systems (IDS) and firewalls. An alternative is TCP SYN scanning, also known as half-open scanning. In this technique, the scanner sends a TCP SYN packet to the target port and waits for a response. If a TCP RST (reset) packet is received, the port is considered closed, and if an ACK (acknowledgment) packet is received, the port is considered open. UDP scanning is another valuable technique used to identify open UDP ports. Unlike TCP, UDP is connectionless, and scanning it requires sending UDP packets to various ports and analyzing the responses. Because UDP does not provide a reliable acknowledgment mechanism, identifying open UDP ports can be challenging and may require additional methods. Stealth scanning techniques are designed to evade detection by intrusion detection systems and firewalls. One such method is the use of fragmented packets, where the scanner sends fragmented IP packets to the target, making it more challenging for network security devices to identify and block the scanning activity. Another technique is the use of idle scanning, where the scanner leverages an already established session to probe the target without initiating direct connections. Idle scanning can help conceal the origin of the scanning activity. Advanced scanning techniques often involve the use of specialized tools and scripts that automate the scanning and enumeration process. For example, the Nmap (Network Mapper) tool is a popular choice among cybersecurity professionals *for conducting comprehensive port scans and enumerating target systems. Nmap provides a wide range of scanning options, including TCP connect scanning, TCP SYN scanning, UDP scanning, and more. It also includes features like version detection to identify specific software and services running on open ports. Banner grabbing is a simple yet effective enumeration technique that involves capturing banners or banners from network services. A banner is a text-based response that some services provide when a connection is established. These banners can reveal valuable information about the service, such as its name, version, and sometimes even vulnerabilities. Service enumeration is the process of identifying the specific services running on open ports. Tools like Nmap can perform service enumeration by analyzing the responses received from open ports and comparing them to a database of known services and their associated ports. Operating system fingerprinting is a valuable technique that allows cybersecurity professionals to identify the target system's underlying operating system. By analyzing subtle differences in the way systems respond to various packets and requests, fingerprinting tools can make educated guesses about the OS in use. Enumeration techniques often extend beyond identifying open ports and services. User enumeration is a common practice in which the attacker attempts to identify valid user accounts on a target system. This can be done through methods like brute-forcing usernames, exploiting misconfigured services, or using social engineering tactics. Share enumeration involves* identifying shared resources on a network, such as file shares, printers, and directories. By identifying accessible shares, attackers can potentially gain unauthorized access to sensitive data. Vulnerability scanning is another essential component of enumeration. Once open ports and services are identified, cybersecurity professionals can use vulnerability scanning tools to check for known security vulnerabilities in those services. Vulnerability scanning helps organizations prioritize security patching and remediation efforts. Enumeration is not limited to external network scanning; it also applies to internal network assessments and penetration testing. Internal enumeration techniques may involve discovering user accounts, group memberships, and privileges, as well as identifying sensitive data repositories and potential attack vectors. The information obtained through enumeration serves as a valuable foundation for penetration testing, where cybersecurity professionals attempt to exploit identified vulnerabilities and assess the overall security posture of the target system or network. In summary, advanced port scanning and enumeration techniques are essential tools in the cybersecurity arsenal. These techniques provide valuable insights into network structures, open ports, and services, helping organizations identify potential vulnerabilities and strengthen their security defenses. Effective port scanning and enumeration require an understanding of various scanning methods, evasion techniques, and specialized tools. By mastering these techniques, cybersecurity professionals can enhance *their ability to assess network security, identify weaknesses, and implement measures to protect against cyber threats.*

In the world of cybersecurity, the journey doesn't end with the initial compromise of a system or network; it is only the beginning. After an attacker gains unauthorized access, the next phase is often post-exploitation, where they aim to maintain control, expand their influence, and achieve their objectives. This chapter explores the intricacies of post-exploitation and how attackers establish persistent access within compromised networks. Post-exploitation encompasses a wide range of activities conducted by attackers after successfully compromising a system. It involves actions such as privilege escalation, data exfiltration, lateral movement within the network, and maintaining access to the compromised system. The primary objective of post-exploitation is to ensure that the attacker retains control and can continue to operate undetected. Privilege escalation is a key aspect of post-exploitation. Once inside a system, attackers seek ways to elevate their privileges, gaining access to more sensitive resources and expanding their reach. This often involves exploiting vulnerabilities or misconfigurations in the operating system or application to gain higher-level access. Password cracking and privilege escalation exploits are common techniques used in this phase. Lateral movement is another critical component of post-exploitation. Attackers want to navigate through the network, hopping from one compromised system to another, searching for valuable information or targets.

This lateral movement can be achieved through techniques like pass-the-hash attacks, where attackers use stolen credentials to move laterally without requiring the original plaintext password. Establishing persistent access is a core objective for attackers during post-exploitation. They want to ensure that even if their initial entry point is discovered and closed, they can still maintain control and access the network. Attackers often install backdoors or create new accounts with elevated privileges to ensure future access. Persistence mechanisms include scheduled tasks, service configuration changes, and registry modifications. Data exfiltration is another crucial aspect of post-exploitation. Once inside a network, attackers aim to extract sensitive information, intellectual property, or other valuable data. Data exfiltration methods vary, including using encrypted tunnels, disguising data as legitimate traffic, or exfiltrating it in small, inconspicuous chunks to evade detection. Steganography, the art of hiding data within other files or media, is a technique often employed for covert data exfiltration. Covering tracks is essential for attackers during post-exploitation. They seek to remove or obfuscate any evidence of their presence, actions, or access within the compromised systems and network. This involves erasing logs, altering timestamps, and ensuring that security personnel or automated systems don't discover their activities. Using anti-forensic techniques, such as rootkit installation and data wiping, can help cover tracks effectively. Advanced attackers may employ rootkits or root-level access to maintain control over compromised systems and hide their *presence from security tools. Maintaining low and slow communication with command and control servers is another technique used to avoid detection. The rise of fileless malware, which resides in memory and doesn't leave traces on disk, has further complicated the detection and analysis of post-exploitation activities. Post-exploitation techniques often leverage legitimate administration and management tools that are already present in the network. Attackers misuse these tools to blend in with normal network traffic and evade detection. For example, PowerShell and Windows Management Instrumentation (WMI) scripts are frequently used for post-exploitation tasks because they are built-in and trusted by system administrators. Living off the land (LotL) is a strategy where attackers use legitimate software and processes that exist within the environment to carry out malicious activities. This makes it challenging for security teams to distinguish between normal operations and post-exploitation actions. Organizations must take proactive steps to detect and mitigate post-exploitation activities. This includes implementing strong network segmentation, monitoring network traffic for anomalous patterns, and using intrusion detection systems (IDS) and intrusion prevention systems (IPS) to identify malicious behavior. User and entity behavior analytics (UEBA) tools can also help identify suspicious activities that deviate from typical user behavior. Intrusion detection and response play a critical role in identifying and mitigating post-exploitation activities. Security teams should have well-defined incident response plans and procedures in place* to respond quickly and effectively to any detected security incidents. This includes isolating compromised systems, conducting forensic analysis, and implementing necessary countermeasures. Effective security awareness training for employees is essential in preventing successful post-exploitation activities. Users should be educated about the risks of social engineering, phishing attacks, and the importance of strong passwords and secure authentication methods. Implementing the principle of least privilege helps limit the damage that can be caused by attackers who successfully exploit vulnerabilities or compromise user accounts. Ensuring that users and systems only have the permissions necessary to perform their specific tasks reduces the attack surface. In summary, post-exploitation is a critical phase in the attacker's playbook, where they seek to maintain control, expand their influence, and achieve their objectives within a compromised network. Understanding the techniques employed during post-exploitation is essential for organizations to detect and mitigate these activities effectively. By implementing strong security measures, monitoring for anomalies, and having robust incident response plans in place, organizations can enhance their ability to detect, respond to, and recover from post-exploitation incidents.

BOOK 3
PENTESTING 101
ADVANCED TECHNIQUES FOR WEB APPLICATION
SECURITY

ROB BOTWRIGHT

Chapter 1: The Landscape of Web Application Security

In the dynamic landscape of cybersecurity, web applications have become integral to our digital lives, from online banking to social media and e-commerce platforms. However, with this increasing reliance on web applications comes a growing risk of security threats and vulnerabilities. This chapter explores the evolving landscape of web application security threats and trends, shedding light on the challenges faced by organizations and individuals alike. Web application security threats pose significant risks to both businesses and individuals, with potential consequences ranging from data breaches to financial losses and reputational damage. One of the most prevalent web application security threats is cross-site scripting (XSS). XSS occurs when an attacker injects malicious scripts into web applications, which are then executed in the context of a user's browser. This can lead to the theft of sensitive information, such as cookies or session tokens, allowing attackers to impersonate users and gain unauthorized access. Another critical threat is SQL injection (SQLi), where attackers manipulate input fields to execute malicious SQL queries against a web application's database. Successful SQL injection attacks can expose sensitive data, modify database contents, or even take control of the underlying server. Web application security threats also extend to insecure authentication mechanisms. Brute-force attacks and credential stuffing are techniques employed by attackers to gain unauthorized access to user accounts by exploiting weak or stolen passwords. Insecure authentication can result in account takeovers, identity theft, and compromised user data. Security misconfigurations are a common web application threat. When developers or administrators fail to configure security settings properly, attackers can exploit these weaknesses to gain unauthorized access or extract sensitive information. Out-of-date software and components are often targeted by attackers. Known vulnerabilities in web application frameworks, libraries, or third-party plugins can be exploited if not promptly patched. File upload vulnerabilities are another threat, allowing attackers to upload malicious files that can compromise the server or execute arbitrary code. API security is a growing concern as more web applications rely on APIs to communicate with external services. Weaknesses in API security can lead to data breaches, unauthorized access, and exposure of sensitive data. Bots and automated attacks pose a significant threat to web applications. Malicious bots can engage in activities such as scraping sensitive data, launching DDoS attacks, or attempting to exploit vulnerabilities at scale. Phishing attacks targeting web applications continue to be a prevalent threat. Attackers use deceptive tactics to trick users into revealing sensitive information, such as login credentials or financial details. As technology evolves, so do the tactics and techniques of web application attackers. One notable trend is the increasing sophistication of attackers, who use advanced tools and techniques to evade detection. They may employ polymorphic malware, obfuscation, and encryption to make their attacks more challenging to detect and analyze. Web application attacks are no longer limited to targeting traditional web browsers. With the rise of mobile applications and Internet of Things (IoT) devices, attackers are adapting their strategies to exploit vulnerabilities in these platforms. Credential stuffing attacks, for example, target reused passwords across various online services, including mobile apps and IoT devices. API security has become a critical focus as organizations adopt microservices and cloud-native architectures. Securing APIs involves not only protecting against traditional attacks but also ensuring that communication between microservices is authenticated, authorized, and encrypted. Serverless applications are also on the rise, introducing new security challenges. Organizations need to consider the security of serverless functions, data storage, and event-driven architectures. The move to the cloud brings both opportunities and challenges in terms of web application security. While cloud providers offer robust security features, organizations must still configure their cloud environments correctly to mitigate risks. DevSecOps is an emerging trend that emphasizes integrating security into the development and deployment pipeline. This approach promotes collaboration between development, operations, and security teams, allowing security to be an integral part of the application lifecycle. In summary, web application security threats and trends continue to evolve, challenging organizations to adapt and strengthen their defenses. Understanding the landscape of web application threats is essential for developing effective security strategies. Organizations must invest in security measures such as secure coding practices, regular vulnerability assessments, and threat intelligence to protect their web applications and user data. By staying informed about emerging threats and adopting proactive security measures, businesses and individuals can mitigate risks and ensure the safety of their web applications in an increasingly interconnected digital world. In today's digital age, web applications are pervasive in our lives, serving as the backbone of countless online services, from email and social media to e-commerce and online banking. While these applications provide unprecedented convenience and functionality, they also introduce significant security risks. Web application security awareness is of paramount importance in safeguarding sensitive data, protecting user privacy, and maintaining the integrity of online services. As the digital landscape continues to evolve, the need for heightened web application security awareness has never been more critical. Web applications are attractive targets for cybercriminals and malicious actors seeking to exploit vulnerabilities for financial gain or other nefarious purposes. One of the key reasons for the heightened importance of web application security awareness is the proliferation of data breaches. Cybercriminals frequently target web applications to steal user data, financial information, and proprietary business data. These breaches can have severe consequences, including financial losses, legal liabilities, and reputational damage. Data breaches not only affect organizations but also impact individuals whose personal information is exposed. The theft of usernames, passwords, and sensitive personal details can lead to identity theft and various forms of online fraud. Another compelling reason to prioritize web application security awareness is the evolving threat landscape. Cyberattacks are becoming increasingly sophisticated, with attackers using a variety of tactics, techniques, and procedures to exploit vulnerabilities.

Advanced persistent threats (APTs), zero-day exploits, and polymorphic malware are just a few examples of the advanced threats facing web applications. Ransomware attacks targeting web applications have also become more prevalent, encrypting critical data and demanding ransom payments for decryption keys. Web application security awareness is crucial in defending against these sophisticated attacks and staying one step ahead of cybercriminals. Web application vulnerabilities can be exploited through a variety of attack vectors, making it imperative for organizations to understand the different types of threats they face. Common web application security vulnerabilities include cross-site scripting (XSS), SQL injection, cross-site request forgery (CSRF), and security misconfigurations. These vulnerabilities can lead to unauthorized access, data leakage, and the compromise of sensitive information. By educating developers, administrators, and users about these vulnerabilities, organizations can take proactive measures to prevent them. Furthermore, web application security is not solely the responsibility of cybersecurity professionals. It requires a collective effort involving developers, system administrators, security teams, and end-users. Developers play a critical role in building secure web applications by following secure coding practices and incorporating security into the development lifecycle. System administrators must configure and maintain web servers, databases, and application platforms securely. Security teams should conduct regular security assessments, vulnerability scanning, and penetration testing to identify and remediate vulnerabilities. End-users, on the other hand, need to practice good security hygiene by using strong, unique passwords, enabling two-factor authentication, and remaining vigilant against phishing and social engineering attacks. Web application security awareness also extends to compliance with industry standards and regulations. Organizations operating in various sectors, such as healthcare, finance, and e-commerce, must adhere to specific compliance requirements, such as the Health Insurance Portability and Accountability Act (HIPAA) or the Payment Card Industry Data Security Standard (PCI DSS). Failure to comply with these regulations can result in fines, legal repercussions, and reputational damage. Awareness of these regulatory requirements and how they relate to web application security is essential for organizations to remain compliant. In addition to protecting sensitive data, web application security is critical for maintaining user trust. Users expect their data to be handled securely, and any breach can erode trust and confidence in an organization's services. A breach can lead to reputational damage that may take years to recover from. Therefore, organizations that prioritize web application security not only protect their data but also preserve their reputation and customer loyalty. Web application security awareness can also help organizations gain a competitive advantage. Security-conscious businesses are more likely to attract customers and partners who value the protection of their data and privacy. Being able to demonstrate a commitment to security through certifications and best practices can set an organization apart in a crowded marketplace. Moreover, organizations that invest in security measures are less likely to incur the financial and operational costs associated with data breaches and security incidents. By proactively addressing vulnerabilities and threats, they can avoid the significant expenses of incident response, data recovery, legal fees, and regulatory fines. Web application security awareness is an ongoing process that requires continuous learning and adaptation. As attackers develop new techniques and exploit emerging vulnerabilities, organizations must stay ahead of the curve. Security awareness training, threat intelligence sharing, and regular security assessments are essential components of a proactive security strategy. In summary, web application security awareness is vital for protecting sensitive data, maintaining user trust, and safeguarding an organization's reputation. The ever-evolving threat landscape demands that organizations prioritize security at every level and involve all stakeholders in the effort to defend against cyberattacks. By investing in security awareness and best practices, organizations can mitigate risks, comply with regulations, and gain a competitive edge in the digital world.

Chapter 2: Understanding Web Application Architecture

A web application is a software program that runs on web servers and interacts with users through web browsers. These applications have become an integral part of our daily lives, enabling us to shop online, access social media, and perform various tasks over the internet. Understanding the components of a typical web application is essential for developers, administrators, and anyone interested in the world of web development. At its core, a web application consists of two primary components: the front-end and the back-end. The front-end, also known as the client-side, is the user interface of the web application that users interact with through their web browsers. It encompasses everything the user sees and interacts with, including web pages, forms, buttons, and other user interface elements. Front-end technologies typically include HTML (Hypertext Markup Language), CSS (Cascading Style Sheets), and JavaScript, which are responsible for rendering web pages, styling them, and adding interactive behavior. Web developers use these technologies to create a visually appealing and user-friendly interface. The back-end, or server-side, is the behind-the-scenes component of a web application responsible for processing requests, managing data, and performing various functions. It includes the web server, application server, and database server. The web server receives incoming HTTP requests from users' browsers and routes them to the appropriate parts of the application. Common web server software includes Apache, Nginx, and Microsoft Internet Information Services (IIS). The application server executes the business logic of the web application, processing requests, handling user authentication, and performing tasks such as retrieving or updating data from the database. Popular application server technologies include Node.js, Ruby on Rails, Django, and Java EE. The database server stores and manages the data required by the web application. It can be a relational database like MySQL, PostgreSQL, or Microsoft SQL Server, or a NoSQL database like MongoDB or Cassandra, depending on the application's requirements. These three components work together to provide the functionality and features of a web application. Beyond the front-end and back-end, a typical web application may also include other components and technologies to enhance its performance, security, and user experience. One such component is a content delivery network (CDN), which helps optimize the delivery of static assets such as images, stylesheets, and JavaScript files. CDNs distribute these assets across multiple geographically dispersed servers to reduce latency and improve loading times for users. Another crucial component is web security mechanisms to protect the application from various threats. This includes measures like authentication and authorization to ensure that only authorized users can access certain parts of the application. Web application firewalls (WAFs) are used to filter and monitor incoming traffic, blocking malicious requests and defending against common web vulnerabilities. Security certificates, such as SSL/TLS certificates, provide encryption to secure data transmission between users' browsers and the web server. In addition to security, web applications often incorporate caching mechanisms to improve performance. Caching involves storing frequently accessed data or pages in temporary memory to reduce the need to retrieve them from the database or generate them dynamically, resulting in faster response times. For example, a web application may cache product listings, reducing the load on the database when multiple users access the same page. Session management is another essential component, allowing web applications to track and maintain user sessions as they navigate through the application. Cookies, tokens, or session IDs are used to identify users and store information about their interactions, such as shopping carts or login status. Scaling is a consideration for web applications that experience increased traffic or growth. Horizontal scaling involves adding more servers to distribute the load, while vertical scaling means increasing the resources (CPU, memory) of existing servers. Load balancers play a vital role in distributing incoming requests evenly across multiple servers to ensure efficient resource utilization and prevent server overload. Monitoring and logging components help administrators track the performance, health, and security of a web application. Logging records events, errors, and user interactions, while monitoring tools track metrics like response times, server load, and resource utilization. These components enable proactive *maintenance, troubleshooting, and performance optimization. In modern web development, web applications often leverage additional technologies and libraries to enhance their functionality. Frameworks like React, Angular, and Vue.js facilitate the development of dynamic and responsive user interfaces. JavaScript libraries, such as jQuery, provide pre-built functions and tools to simplify client-side scripting. APIs (Application Programming Interfaces) allow web applications to interact with external services, such as payment gateways, social media platforms, or mapping services. Microservices architecture, a growing trend, decomposes web applications into smaller, loosely coupled services that can be developed and deployed independently. This approach improves scalability, maintainability, and flexibility. Progressive Web Apps (PWAs) are web applications that combine the best of web and mobile app experiences, providing offline access, push notifications, and a more native-like user experience. Web components, a set of web platform APIs and specifications, enable the creation of reusable, encapsulated custom elements that enhance modularity and maintainability. Web application development tools, integrated development environments (IDEs), version control systems, and continuous integration/continuous deployment (CI/CD) pipelines are essential for streamlining the development, testing, and deployment processes. Cloud platforms, such as AWS, Azure, and Google Cloud, offer scalable infrastructure and services for hosting web applications, reducing the operational burden on organizations. In summary, web* applications are complex software systems consisting of front-end and back-end components that work together to provide functionality, security, and a seamless user experience. Understanding the various components and technologies involved is essential for developers, administrators, and stakeholders involved in web application development and maintenance. As web technologies continue to evolve, staying informed about emerging trends and best practices is crucial for building and maintaining successful web applications that meet the needs of users in an ever-changing digital landscape. Web application development is a dynamic field that continuously evolves with emerging technologies and frameworks. These tools and technologies empower developers to create powerful, interactive, and responsive web applications that cater to diverse user needs. Next, we delve into the world of web application development frameworks and technologies, exploring the essential components that drive the development process. One of the foundational elements of web application development is the programming language. Several languages are commonly used, with JavaScript being the primary language for front-end development. JavaScript allows developers to add dynamic behavior to web pages, making them interactive and responsive to user actions. On the server-side, languages like Python, Ruby, PHP, Java, and Node.js are frequently used to build the back-end logic of web applications. These languages provide the necessary tools and libraries for handling HTTP requests, managing databases, and executing server-side operations. Web development *frameworks serve as the scaffolding that streamlines the development process by providing pre-built code and structure. For front-end development, popular frameworks like React, Angular, and Vue.js enable developers to create reusable components and manage the state of their applications efficiently. These frameworks facilitate the creation of modern, responsive, and user-friendly interfaces. On the server-side, frameworks such as Ruby on Rails, Django, and Express.js simplify the development of back-end logic. They provide features like routing, authentication, and database interaction out of the box, allowing developers to focus on application-specific functionality. Databases are a critical component of web applications for storing and managing data. Relational databases like MySQL, PostgreSQL, and Microsoft SQL Server are commonly used for structured data, while NoSQL databases like MongoDB and Cassandra excel at handling unstructured or semi-structured data. The choice of database technology depends on the application's data requirements and scalability needs. Web application development often involves integrating with external services and APIs (Application Programming Interfaces). APIs enable web applications to interact with services such as payment gateways, social media platforms, and mapping services. Authentication services like OAuth and OpenID Connect allow users to log in using their credentials from other trusted providers, simplifying the authentication process and enhancing security. RESTful APIs and GraphQL provide standardized approaches for defining and accessing data over HTTP, enabling efficient communication between web applications and external services. Serverless architecture is gaining popularity in web development, allowing developers to build and deploy applications without managing traditional servers. Platforms like AWS Lambda and Azure Functions enable the execution of code in response to events, such as HTTP requests or database changes, without the need for server maintenance. This approach offers scalability and cost savings, as organizations only pay for the compute resources they use. Microservices architecture is another trend in web application development, emphasizing the decomposition of applications into smaller, independently deployable services. Each microservice focuses on a specific business function and communicates with others through APIs. This architecture promotes modularity, scalability, and flexibility, allowing teams to develop, deploy, and maintain services autonomously. Front-end development tools and libraries play a crucial role in creating responsive and engaging user interfaces. Libraries like jQuery simplify DOM manipulation and AJAX requests, while CSS frameworks like Bootstrap and Foundation provide pre-designed UI components and responsive layouts. Front-end build tools such as Webpack and Babel enable developers to bundle, transpile, and optimize their JavaScript code for production. Web components, a set of web platform APIs and specifications, allow developers to create custom HTML elements with encapsulated functionality. These components promote reusability and maintainability in large-scale web applications. Progressive Web Apps (PWAs) are a hybrid approach that combines the best of web and mobile application experiences. PWAs provide features such as offline access, push notifications, and improved performance, making them feel more like native apps. They leverage technologies like service workers to cache content and respond to network requests, ensuring a seamless user experience. Web security is a critical consideration in web application development. Developers must address common security vulnerabilities such as cross-site scripting (XSS), SQL injection, and cross-site request forgery (CSRF). Security frameworks and libraries, such as OWASP (Open Web Application Security Project) recommendations and security headers, help developers secure their applications against these threats. Web application firewalls (WAFs) provide an additional layer of security, monitoring and filtering incoming traffic to block malicious requests. Secure coding practices, regular security assessments, and penetration testing are essential for identifying and mitigating security risks. In the ever-evolving landscape of web application development, staying up-to-date with emerging technologies and best practices is crucial. Developers should continually explore new frameworks, tools, and methodologies to enhance their skills and deliver innovative, secure, and user-friendly web applications. Web development communities, online resources, and forums provide valuable insights and support for developers seeking to excel in this dynamic field. In summary, web application development is a multifaceted discipline that encompasses a wide range of programming languages, frameworks, and technologies. These components work together to create responsive, secure, and feature-rich web applications that cater to the needs of users in an increasingly digital world. Web developers must adapt to the evolving landscape, embracing new tools and best practices to deliver high-quality web applications that meet the demands of modern users.*

Chapter 3: Web Application Reconnaissance and Information Gathering

Before embarking on the development of a web application, it's crucial to gather essential information that lays the foundation for a successful project. This phase is often referred to as the discovery or requirements gathering phase, and it sets the stage for understanding the project's objectives, constraints, and user needs. The first step in gathering information about web applications involves identifying the project's stakeholders and decision-makers. Understanding who will be involved in the project and who has the authority to make critical decisions is essential for effective communication and project management. Stakeholders may include the client or organization commissioning the project, end-users, product owners, project managers, developers, designers, and quality assurance teams. Once the stakeholders are identified, the next step is to conduct initial meetings or interviews to gain a deeper understanding of the project's goals and objectives. These discussions provide an opportunity to clarify the project's scope, requirements, and constraints. It's essential to ask open-ended questions and actively listen to stakeholders' input to uncover valuable insights. During these conversations, you should aim to identify the project's target audience or user base. Understanding the demographics, needs, and preferences of the intended users helps tailor the application to their expectations and requirements. User personas, created based on this information, can serve as a valuable reference throughout the development process. Another critical aspect of gathering information is identifying the business or organizational goals that the web application aims to achieve. These goals could be related to revenue generation, brand awareness, process optimization, or providing specific services to users. Clearly defining these objectives ensures that the web application aligns with the broader mission and strategy of the organization. Defining the project's scope is a crucial step in information gathering. Scope documentation outlines the features, functionalities, and boundaries of the web application. It helps prevent scope creep, where additional requirements are introduced after the project has commenced, which can lead to delays and budget overruns. To gather technical information about the web application, it's essential to understand the existing technology stack, infrastructure, and any legacy systems that may need to be integrated or replaced. Assessing the organization's current technical environment provides insights into compatibility, data migration, and system integration challenges. Understanding the competitive landscape is also vital. Researching competitors and similar web applications in the market helps identify opportunities for differentiation and innovation. Analyzing competitors' strengths and weaknesses can inform strategic decisions and help position the web application effectively. User experience (UX) research and design are integral parts of gathering information about web applications. UX research involves understanding user behavior, preferences, pain points, and expectations through methods like user surveys, usability testing, and user interviews. This data guides the design process, ensuring that the web application is user-centric and intuitive. Wireframing and prototyping are tools used in the design phase to visualize the application's layout, navigation, and user interface. They serve as a blueprint for the development team and provide stakeholders with a clear vision of the final product. Accessibility considerations are also important during the information gathering phase. Ensuring that the web application is accessible to users with disabilities is not only a legal requirement in many regions but also a crucial aspect of inclusivity and usability. Compliance with web accessibility standards such as WCAG (Web Content Accessibility Guidelines) is essential. Security is a paramount concern in web application development, and gathering information about potential security threats and vulnerabilities is crucial. Conducting a security assessment and identifying security requirements early in the process can help prevent data breaches and other security incidents. Scalability and performance requirements should also be addressed during the information gathering phase. Understanding the expected traffic volume, concurrent users, and response time requirements helps in designing a scalable and responsive architecture. Regulatory and compliance considerations may vary depending on the industry and region in which the web application operates. Gathering information about applicable regulations and compliance requirements ensures that *the application meets legal and industry-specific standards. Budget and resource constraints are essential considerations during this phase. Understanding the budget available for the project and the availability of resources, including personnel, tools, and technology, helps set realistic expectations and plan accordingly. Project timelines and milestones should be defined during the information gathering phase. Establishing a project schedule with clear deliverables and deadlines ensures that the development process stays on track and aligns with the project's objectives. Risk assessment is another crucial aspect of gathering information. Identifying potential risks, their impact, and mitigation strategies allows the project team to proactively address challenges that may arise during development. Finally, documentation is a critical output of the information gathering phase. All the information collected, including stakeholder requirements, technical specifications, user personas, and design concepts, should be documented in a comprehensive project brief or requirements document. This document serves as a reference point for all project stakeholders and guides the development team throughout the project's lifecycle. In summary, gathering information about web applications is a foundational step in the development process. It involves understanding the project's stakeholders, goals, scope, technical requirements, user needs, and constraints. By conducting thorough research and documentation during this phase, development teams can lay the groundwork for a successful web application that meets both user expectations and organizational objectives. Effective information gathering sets the stage for efficient project planning, design, development, and ultimately, the delivery of a valuable web application to users and clients. In the realm of ethical hacking and penetration testing, the first critical step is to identify potential targets and attack surfaces within the target organization. This phase involves a systematic approach to discover vulnerabilities and weaknesses that malicious attackers might exploit. The objective is to assess the security posture of the organization's digital assets and infrastructure, helping it proactively address vulnerabilities and enhance security. Identifying targets begins with gaining a comprehensive understanding of the target organization's digital footprint. This includes all the assets, resources, and online presence that could be potential targets for attacks. Typically, organizations have a variety of digital assets, ranging from web applications and servers to databases, network devices, and even employee endpoints. A critical aspect of this phase is to identify and catalog all the public-facing assets. These are the assets accessible from the internet and, therefore, susceptible to external attacks. Public-facing assets often include websites, web applications, email servers, and any services accessible through public IP addresses. To discover these assets, ethical hackers use various techniques, such as passive reconnaissance and active reconnaissance. Passive reconnaissance involves collecting information about the target organization without directly interacting with its systems. This can include searching for public information on the internet, analyzing DNS records, and reviewing publicly available documents and reports. Active reconnaissance, on the other hand, involves direct interactions with the target systems to gather information. Common methods include port scanning, DNS enumeration, and banner grabbing. The goal is to identify open ports, services, and software versions running on the target systems. Once the public-facing assets are identified, the next step is to enumerate the attack surfaces associated with these assets. An attack surface is the set of entry points and vulnerabilities that attackers can potentially exploit to compromise a system or application. Web applications, for instance, have specific attack surfaces that include input fields, APIs, authentication mechanisms, and the underlying database. Enumerating attack surfaces involves mapping out the functionalities and interactions of the application, understanding how user input is processed, and identifying potential vulnerabilities. In the case of network devices, the attack surface may encompass open ports, protocols, and any exposed management interfaces. To identify vulnerabilities in web applications, ethical hackers often utilize automated scanning tools and manual testing techniques. Automated scanners can help identify common vulnerabilities, such as SQL injection, cross-site scripting (XSS), and insecure configurations. However, manual testing is crucial for uncovering complex vulnerabilities and logic flaws that automated tools might miss. The process of identifying attack surfaces also extends to network infrastructure. Ethical hackers examine the* network topology, identifying routers, switches, firewalls, and other devices that could be potential targets. They analyze network protocols, configurations, and access controls to assess the security of the network. This phase of enumeration and identification requires meticulous attention to detail and a deep understanding of network and application security principles. The ultimate goal is to create a comprehensive inventory of the attack surfaces, vulnerabilities, and potential entry points that could be exploited by malicious actors. In addition to external attack surfaces, ethical hackers must also consider internal attack vectors. These are potential vulnerabilities and weaknesses within the organization's internal network that could be exploited by insiders or attackers who have gained access to the network. Internal attack surfaces may include poorly configured servers, outdated software, weak access controls, and unpatched systems. To identify internal vulnerabilities, ethical hackers often conduct internal network assessments, including vulnerability scanning, password auditing, and privilege escalation testing. In some cases, organizations also engage in social engineering tests to assess the human element of security, as employees can unwittingly become attack vectors. Once all the potential targets and attack surfaces are identified, ethical hackers prioritize them based on their criticality and potential impact. This prioritization helps organizations focus their resources and efforts on addressing the most significant security risks first. It's essential to consider both the technical severity of *vulnerabilities and their relevance to the organization's business goals. A critical vulnerability in a system that holds sensitive customer data, for example, should be addressed with the utmost urgency. Finally, ethical hackers document their findings and present them to the organization in a detailed report. This report typically includes a list of identified vulnerabilities, their severity, potential impact, and recommendations for remediation. The report provides organizations with a roadmap for improving their security posture and addressing the identified weaknesses. In summary, the process of identifying targets and attack surfaces is a critical phase in ethical hacking and penetration testing. It involves discovering all potential entry points, vulnerabilities, and weaknesses that could be exploited by attackers. Through meticulous reconnaissance and assessment, ethical hackers provide organizations with valuable insights to enhance their security and protect their digital assets. This proactive approach is essential in today's threat landscape, where cyberattacks continue to evolve and pose significant risks to organizations of all sizes.*

Chapter 4: Cross-Site Scripting (XSS) Attacks and Defenses

Cross-Site Scripting (XSS) attacks are a prevalent and dangerous type of web application vulnerability that allows attackers to inject malicious scripts into web pages viewed by other users. XSS attacks can have various forms and manifestations, making them a significant concern for web developers and security professionals. Next, we'll explore the different types of XSS attacks and the payloads that attackers use to exploit them. XSS attacks can be categorized into three main types: Stored XSS, Reflected XSS, and DOM-based XSS. Stored XSS occurs when an attacker injects a malicious script, which gets permanently stored on the target server and served to other users who view the affected page. Attackers often exploit vulnerabilities in user-generated content, such as comments, forum posts, or user profiles, to inject their malicious payloads. Reflected XSS, on the other hand, involves injecting a malicious script into a web page, which is then reflected off the server to the victim's browser. This type of XSS attack typically relies on tricking users into clicking on a malicious link containing the payload. DOM-based XSS attacks take advantage of vulnerabilities in client-side scripts that manipulate the Document Object Model (DOM) of a web page. Attackers can inject payloads that manipulate the DOM and execute malicious code in the user's browser. To effectively defend against XSS attacks, it's crucial to understand the various payloads that attackers use to exploit vulnerabilities. One common payload is the script tag itself, which allows attackers to execute arbitrary JavaScript code within the victim's browser. Attackers may also employ event handlers, such as onload or onmouseover, to trigger malicious actions when a user interacts with the page. Payloads can be obfuscated or encoded to evade security filters and detection mechanisms. For example, attackers may use JavaScript encoding techniques like hexadecimal encoding or base64 encoding to hide their payloads. Another payload type involves injecting malicious code that steals user data, such as cookies or session tokens, and sends it to the attacker-controlled server. This data theft can lead to session hijacking and unauthorized access to user accounts. XSS payloads can also be used for defacement attacks, where attackers manipulate the page's content to display offensive or malicious messages to other users. In some cases, attackers inject payloads that redirect users to phishing sites or malicious domains, aiming to steal credentials or spread malware. Beaconing payloads are another category used by attackers to notify them when a user has fallen victim to an XSS attack. These payloads silently send information to an external server, allowing attackers to track successful exploits. To mitigate XSS attacks, web developers and organizations should implement security best practices and employ various security mechanisms. Input validation and output encoding are essential steps in preventing XSS vulnerabilities. Developers should validate and sanitize user input to ensure that it doesn't contain malicious code. Additionally, output encoding should be applied when rendering user-generated content to prevent the execution of injected scripts. Content Security Policy (CSP) headers can help mitigate XSS attacks by specifying which domains are allowed to execute scripts on a web page. CSP provides an added layer of security by limiting the sources from which scripts can be loaded, reducing the attack surface for XSS vulnerabilities. Web application firewalls (WAFs) can also help detect and block malicious payloads and requests that may exploit XSS vulnerabilities. Regular security testing, including vulnerability scanning and penetration testing, is crucial to identifying and addressing XSS vulnerabilities before attackers can exploit them. Security education and awareness training for developers and users can help raise awareness of the risks associated with XSS attacks and promote secure coding practices. In summary, XSS attacks remain a significant threat to web applications and their users. Understanding the various types of XSS attacks and the payloads used by attackers is essential for effective defense. By implementing security measures such as input validation, output encoding, and Content Security Policy, organizations can reduce the risk of XSS vulnerabilities and protect their users from malicious exploitation. Security awareness and regular testing are vital components of a comprehensive security strategy, helping to stay one step ahead of attackers in the ever-evolving landscape of web application security. Protecting web applications against Cross-Site Scripting (XSS) vulnerabilities is a critical aspect of web security, and there are several best practices and techniques that developers and organizations can employ to mitigate the risk of XSS attacks. XSS attacks occur when malicious scripts are injected into web pages and executed by a user's browser, potentially compromising the user's data and security. To defend against XSS vulnerabilities, developers should implement proper input validation and output encoding. Input validation involves checking and sanitizing user-generated data before it's processed by the application. This can prevent attackers from injecting malicious scripts in the first place. For instance, if an input field is supposed to accept only numeric values, any non-numeric characters should be rejected or sanitized. Output encoding, on the other hand, is crucial when rendering user-generated content in web pages. All user-generated content, such as comments, forum posts, or user profiles, should be sanitized and encoded to ensure that any potentially malicious code within the content doesn't execute when displayed. One common technique is HTML entity encoding, where characters like "<" and ">" are replaced with their respective HTML entities. Content Security Policy (CSP) is an essential security feature that can mitigate XSS vulnerabilities. CSP allows website owners to define a policy that specifies which domains are allowed to execute scripts on a web page. By restricting the sources from which scripts can be loaded, CSP reduces the attack surface for XSS attacks. For example, a CSP policy can prevent scripts from being executed if they are loaded from an external domain not explicitly permitted in the policy. Web application firewalls (WAFs) can provide an additional layer of defense against XSS attacks. WAFs inspect incoming traffic to a web application and can block requests that contain malicious payloads or patterns commonly associated with XSS attacks. Regularly updating and patching web application software and frameworks is essential to prevent known vulnerabilities that attackers might exploit for XSS attacks. Developers should stay informed about security updates and apply them promptly. Secure development practices, such as following the principles of least privilege and practicing proper session management, are fundamental to XSS mitigation. Developers should ensure that their applications only request and utilize the permissions and data necessary for their functionality. Additionally, web sessions should be securely managed, and session tokens should be protected from theft and exploitation. Properly configuring security headers can help mitigate XSS vulnerabilities. HTTP headers like the X-Content-Type-Options header and the X-XSS-Protection header provide additional security controls. The X-Content-Type-Options header prevents browsers from interpreting files as a different MIME type, reducing the risk of content sniffing attacks. The X-XSS-Protection header enables the browser's built-in XSS filter, adding an extra layer of protection. Security awareness and training for developers and all personnel involved in web application development are crucial. Educating teams about common XSS attack vectors, vulnerabilities, and best practices can help prevent the introduction of vulnerabilities during the development process. Regular security testing, including automated vulnerability scanning and manual penetration testing, is essential to identify and remediate XSS vulnerabilities. Automated scanning tools can detect known vulnerabilities, while manual testing can uncover complex or unique vulnerabilities that automated tools may miss. Input validation, output encoding, and other security measures should be periodically reviewed and tested to ensure they remain effective. Security incident response plans should be in place to address any successful XSS attacks quickly. In the event of an attack, organizations should have a well-defined process for isolating the affected system, investigating the incident, and applying necessary fixes. Logging and monitoring are essential for detecting and responding to XSS attacks in real-time. Monitoring user activities, server logs, and network traffic can help identify suspicious behavior and potential attacks. Regularly reviewing and analyzing logs can lead to early detection and mitigation of XSS threats. When developing web applications, developers should use frameworks and libraries that provide built-in security features for XSS prevention. Many modern frameworks offer template engines and input validation functions designed to protect against common vulnerabilities. However, it's crucial for developers to understand how these features work and to use them correctly. In summary, mitigating XSS vulnerabilities is a fundamental aspect of web application security. By implementing input validation, output encoding, Content Security Policy, and other security best practices, organizations can reduce the risk of XSS *attacks. Regular updates, security headers, and security awareness training are additional layers of defense against XSS threats. Monitoring, incident response planning, and secure development practices round out a comprehensive strategy for protecting web applications and their users from XSS vulnerabilities.*

Chapter 5: SQL Injection and Database Security

SQL injection is a widespread and dangerous web application vulnerability that allows attackers to manipulate a web application's database queries. By injecting malicious SQL code into user input fields or other vulnerable areas, attackers can execute arbitrary SQL commands, potentially compromising the application's data and security. To effectively defend against SQL injection attacks, it's essential to understand the various exploitation techniques employed by attackers. The UNION-based SQL injection technique is one of the most common methods used by attackers. In a UNION-based attack, the attacker leverages the SQL UNION operator to combine the results of two or more SQL queries into a single result set. The goal is to extract data from the database that the application does not intend to disclose. Attackers typically identify vulnerable points in the application where their input is included in database queries without proper sanitization. For example, if a web application uses URL parameters in database queries without adequate input validation and sanitation, it can become a target for UNION-based SQL injection. The attacker crafts a malicious input that includes a UNION statement with additional queries to extract data. Blind SQL injection is another technique used when the application doesn't directly display database errors. In a blind SQL injection attack, attackers infer the presence or absence of data by sending specially crafted payloads and observing the application's behavior. There are two main types of blind SQL injection: boolean-based and time-based. Boolean-based blind SQL injection relies on the application's response to true or false conditions. The attacker sends payloads that evaluate conditions, such as whether a specific character in a database column exists or not. Based on the application's response, the attacker deduces information about the database. Time-based blind SQL injection, on the other hand, introduces delays in the SQL queries to infer data. Attackers send payloads that cause the database to pause for a specified amount of time if a condition is true. By measuring the time it takes for the application to respond, attackers can determine if their injected conditions are valid. Error-based SQL injection is a technique that relies on exposing detailed error messages generated by the database. When an attacker injects malicious input that causes a SQL error, the database may respond with an error message that contains valuable information, such as the database type and structure. This information can help attackers fine-tune their SQL injection payloads. Out-of-band SQL injection is used when an attacker cannot directly retrieve data from the database. In this technique, the attacker sends data to an external server controlled by them. This data may include sensitive information from the database. Out-of-band SQL injection is typically employed when the application's security controls prevent attackers from directly retrieving data. Time-based blind SQL injection payloads can be used to trigger the out-of-band data transmission. Second-order

SQL injection, also known as stored or persistent SQL injection, occurs when the malicious payload is stored in the application's database and executed at a later time. In these attacks, the attacker first injects the payload into the application, which stores it in the database. The payload is then executed when a legitimate user interacts with the application, leading to data exposure or manipulation. To mitigate SQL injection vulnerabilities, developers should adopt secure coding practices. Input validation and parameterized queries are essential techniques to prevent SQL injection. Input validation ensures that user input adheres to expected formats and values, while parameterized queries separate SQL code from user input, making it impossible for attackers to inject malicious SQL. Web application firewalls (WAFs) can help detect and block SQL injection attempts by monitoring incoming traffic for suspicious patterns and payloads. Regularly updating and patching the application's software, including the database management system, helps eliminate known vulnerabilities that attackers might exploit. Developers should follow security guidelines for their chosen programming languages and frameworks to ensure secure coding practices. Security testing, including manual code review and automated scanning, can help identify and remediate SQL injection vulnerabilities before attackers can exploit them. Web application security training and awareness programs can educate developers and organizations about the risks associated with SQL injection and the best practices for prevention. In summary, SQL injection is a prevalent and dangerous web application vulnerability. Attackers employ various techniques, including UNION-based, blind, error-based, out-of-band, and second-order SQL injection, to exploit this vulnerability. Developers and organizations must prioritize secure coding practices, input validation, parameterized queries, and regular software updates to mitigate SQL injection risks effectively. Web application firewalls and security testing play crucial roles in detecting and preventing SQL injection attacks, while security awareness programs help educate stakeholders about the importance of web application security. Securing databases is a paramount concern for organizations that rely on these data repositories to store sensitive information, and there are various security measures and countermeasures that organizations can implement to protect their databases from threats and breaches. A well-designed database security strategy encompasses multiple layers of defense, starting with access control and authentication. Access control ensures that only authorized individuals or applications can interact with the database. Authentication mechanisms, such as username and password, two-factor authentication, or biometrics, verify the identity of users before granting them access. Implementing strong and complex password policies can thwart brute-force attacks and unauthorized access attempts. Role-based access control (RBAC) is an effective way to manage permissions and privileges within the database. RBAC assigns roles to users or groups, defining what actions they can perform on specific database objects. By using

RBAC, organizations can enforce the principle of least privilege, ensuring that users only have the access necessary to perform their job functions. Database encryption is another critical security measure to protect data at rest and in transit. Data at rest encryption ensures that data stored on disk is unreadable without the appropriate decryption key. Data in transit encryption secures data as it travels between the database server and client applications. Secure Sockets Layer (SSL) or Transport Layer Security (TLS) protocols are commonly used for data in transit encryption. Encrypting sensitive data fields, such as credit card numbers or Social Security numbers, within the database adds an extra layer of protection, even if an attacker gains access to the database. Regularly patching and updating the database management system (DBMS) is essential to address known vulnerabilities that attackers might exploit. DBMS vendors release patches and updates to fix security issues and improve overall system stability. To maintain a secure database environment, organizations must stay informed about these updates and apply them promptly. Database auditing and monitoring play a crucial role in identifying suspicious activities and potential security breaches. Auditing records database events, such as logins, data modifications, and privilege changes. These audit logs are essential for forensic analysis and compliance with security regulations. Database monitoring involves real-time analysis of database activity to detect anomalies or deviations from normal behavior. Anomaly detection mechanisms can raise alerts or trigger automated responses to mitigate threats. Implementing data masking or redaction techniques can protect sensitive information from unauthorized access. Data masking replaces sensitive data with fictional or scrambled values, ensuring that real data remains hidden. Redaction selectively removes or obscures sensitive information in database queries or reports, allowing organizations to share data without revealing confidential details. Database activity monitoring (DAM) solutions can provide real-time visibility into database activities and help organizations detect and respond to threats promptly. Regularly reviewing and analyzing audit logs and monitoring data are essential components of a comprehensive database security strategy. Database security also extends to securing backups and ensuring their availability and integrity. Backups should be stored in secure locations and encrypted to prevent data exposure if they fall into the wrong hands. Organizations should regularly test their backup and recovery processes to ensure that they can quickly restore data in case of a breach or data loss. SQL injection attacks are a significant threat to database security, and organizations must take steps to mitigate this risk. By validating and sanitizing user input, developers can prevent attackers from injecting malicious SQL code into application queries. Web application firewalls (WAFs) can help detect and block SQL injection attempts at the application layer. Database security policies and procedures are critical to maintaining a secure database environment. These policies define rules and guidelines for managing and protecting data. They cover areas such as access control, data classification, data retention, and incident response. Training and educating employees about these policies are essential to ensure compliance and best practices. Database administrators should follow the principle of least privilege, granting users and applications only the permissions they need to perform their tasks. Regularly reviewing and revoking unnecessary privileges can reduce the attack surface and the risk of unauthorized access. Database security should also consider the physical security of database servers and storage devices. Physical access controls, surveillance, and environmental controls can prevent unauthorized individuals from physically tampering with or stealing hardware. Organizations should have an incident response plan in place to address security breaches promptly. The plan should outline procedures for identifying and containing the breach, notifying affected parties, and conducting forensic analysis. In summary, securing databases is a multifaceted endeavor that requires a combination of technical measures, policies, and best practices. Access control, authentication, encryption, and auditing are essential security measures to protect data integrity and confidentiality. Regular patching, monitoring, and backup strategies are equally vital to maintaining a robust database security posture. By implementing these measures and following security policies and procedures, organizations can reduce the risk of data breaches and protect their valuable assets.

Chapter 6: Authentication and Session Management Testing

Testing the authentication mechanisms of a web application is a critical step in evaluating its overall security posture. Authentication is the process of verifying the identity of users or entities trying to access a system or application. It is the first line of defense against unauthorized access and is essential for protecting sensitive data and resources. Properly configured and robust authentication mechanisms are crucial for ensuring that only legitimate users can interact with an application. However, if authentication is flawed or vulnerable, attackers can exploit these weaknesses to gain unauthorized access, potentially leading to data breaches and security incidents. Therefore, thorough testing of authentication mechanisms is essential to identify and remediate vulnerabilities before they can be exploited by malicious actors. One of the primary goals of testing authentication mechanisms is to verify that user credentials, such as usernames and passwords, are adequately protected. Credentials should be stored securely using strong cryptographic hashing algorithms. Testing should include verifying that passwords are hashed and salted before storage to prevent attackers from easily cracking them. Salted hashes ensure that even if two users have the same password, their hashed representations are different, adding an extra layer of security. A common testing approach is to attempt to crack hashed passwords using dictionary attacks, brute-force attacks, or rainbow tables. These attacks simulate what an attacker might do if they gained access to the password hashes. A robust authentication mechanism should withstand such attacks. Testing should also check for common vulnerabilities like SQL injection or other injection attacks that might bypass authentication by manipulating the input fields. For example, attackers may attempt to log in using SQL injection to extract data or gain unauthorized access. Implementing proper input validation and sanitation is crucial to prevent injection attacks. Session management is another crucial aspect of authentication testing. Sessions should be securely managed to prevent session fixation, session hijacking, or session fixation attacks. Testing should include checking for weak session IDs, ensuring that sessions are invalidated after logout, and verifying that session tokens are protected from theft. Testing should also evaluate the effectiveness of account lockout mechanisms. Account lockout helps protect against brute-force attacks by temporarily locking user accounts after a specified number of failed login attempts. Testers should attempt to trigger account lockouts by repeatedly entering incorrect credentials and verify that the mechanism functions as intended. Two-factor authentication (2FA) and multi-factor authentication (MFA) should be thoroughly tested to ensure that they provide the expected level of security. Testing should include validating that the second factor (such as a one-time password or biometric data) is required and properly verified during login. Implementing security *headers, such as HTTP Strict Transport Security (HSTS) and X-Content-Type-Options, can enhance authentication security. Testing should ensure that these headers are correctly configured to prevent common web vulnerabilities like clickjacking and content sniffing. Testing should also evaluate the handling of user session timeouts and idle timeouts. Session timeout settings should log users out after a period of inactivity to reduce the risk of unauthorized access if a user leaves their session unattended. It's essential to confirm that users are logged out as expected when their session times out. Testing should consider the handling of error messages during the authentication process. Error messages should not reveal sensitive information, such as whether a username or password is incorrect. Attackers can use such information to guess valid usernames and passwords. Testing should verify that generic error messages are displayed instead of specific error details. Brute-force protection mechanisms should be examined to determine if they effectively prevent attackers from conducting automated attacks. These mechanisms may include CAPTCHA challenges, delays between login attempts, or other rate-limiting techniques. Testing should attempt to bypass these protections and assess their robustness. Testing should also evaluate the account recovery and password reset processes. These processes should be secure and require users to provide sufficient proof of identity before allowing them to reset their passwords or recover their accounts. Authentication testing should encompass both positive and negative testing scenarios. Positive testing verifies that the authentication mechanism works as expected when valid credentials are provided. Negative testing focuses on attempting to break or bypass authentication using various attack vectors and invalid inputs. Testing should include different types of users, such as regular users, administrators, and privileged users, to ensure that access controls are properly enforced. Testing should encompass all authentication methods supported by the application, including local authentication, third-party identity providers (e.g., OAuth or SAML), and single sign-on (SSO) solutions. The testing process should document and report any identified vulnerabilities, providing details on the nature of the vulnerability, the steps to reproduce it, and potential impacts. Vulnerabilities should be prioritized based on their severity and the potential risks they pose. Upon identifying vulnerabilities, remediation efforts should be initiated promptly. This may involve implementing code fixes, configuration changes, or updates to authentication mechanisms. Testing should be conducted periodically, especially after significant changes to the authentication process or application. It's important to ensure that new features or updates do not introduce vulnerabilities or weaken existing security controls. External security assessments, such as penetration testing or third-party security audits, can provide an objective evaluation of authentication mechanisms. These assessments bring an independent perspective and can uncover vulnerabilities that may be overlooked by in-house testing. In summary, testing authentication mechanisms is a crucial aspect of web* application security. It involves a comprehensive evaluation of password security, input validation, session management, error handling, and various attack vectors. Regular and thorough testing helps organizations identify and address authentication vulnerabilities, reducing the risk of unauthorized access and data breaches.

Session management is a fundamental component of web application security, responsible for maintaining user-specific information and providing a seamless experience during user interactions with the application. However, session management can be vulnerable to various security threats that, if not properly addressed, can lead to unauthorized access, data breaches, and other security incidents. Understanding these vulnerabilities and implementing safeguards is essential to maintain the integrity of user sessions and protect sensitive data. One common session management vulnerability is session fixation, where an attacker sets or hijacks a user's session ID, enabling them to impersonate the user and gain unauthorized access. To safeguard against session fixation, web applications should generate a unique session ID for each user upon login and invalidate any existing session IDs. Additionally, it's crucial to use secure and unpredictable session IDs that cannot be easily guessed or brute-forced by attackers. Session hijacking, also known as session theft or session sidejacking, occurs when an attacker intercepts or steals a user's session token, allowing them to assume the user's identity and access their account. To mitigate session hijacking, it's essential to use secure transport protocols like HTTPS to encrypt data in transit and protect session tokens from interception. Implementing secure cookies with the "HttpOnly" and "Secure" flags can further enhance session security by preventing client-side script access and ensuring that cookies are transmitted over secure channels only. Session fixation and session hijacking are often interconnected, as session fixation can set the stage for subsequent session hijacking. To prevent session fixation and hijacking, applications should regenerate session IDs upon successful login, effectively invalidating any previously set session IDs. Another session management vulnerability is session timeout manipulation, where an attacker extends the lifetime of their own session or that of another user. Attackers may achieve this by manipulating session cookies, modifying expiration times, or using various techniques to keep sessions alive beyond their intended duration. To safeguard against session timeout manipulation, developers should ensure that sessions expire after a reasonable period of inactivity, and users must reauthenticate when their session expires. Furthermore, implementing a robust idle timeout mechanism ensures that sessions are automatically terminated if users remain inactive for an extended period. Cross-Site Request Forgery (CSRF) is a security threat that targets session management by tricking users into performing unwanted actions on authenticated websites without their consent. Attackers may craft malicious requests that execute actions on behalf of the user, such as changing account settings or making unauthorized transactions. To defend against

CSRF attacks, web applications should employ anti-CSRF tokens that are unique to each user session and verified with every sensitive action. These tokens ensure that requests originate from the legitimate user and are not forged by malicious entities. Session data stored on the client side, such as in cookies or local storage, can be vulnerable to tampering by attackers, leading to session manipulation. Attackers may attempt to modify session variables, such as user roles or permissions, to escalate privileges or gain unauthorized access to protected resources. To prevent session data tampering, developers should use integrity checks or digital signatures to verify the authenticity and integrity of session data on the server side. Session fixation, session hijacking, and CSRF attacks can be challenging to detect solely through manual code review or static analysis. Therefore, implementing robust security testing practices, such as dynamic application security testing (DAST) and penetration testing, is crucial to identify and remediate session management vulnerabilities. Automated scanners and manual testing can help uncover security weaknesses and validate the effectiveness of session safeguards. Web application firewalls (WAFs) can provide additional protection by inspecting incoming requests and blocking potentially malicious traffic that may exploit session vulnerabilities. Regular security assessments and vulnerability scans should be conducted to stay ahead of evolving threats and emerging vulnerabilities. Education and awareness play a vital role in mitigating session management vulnerabilities. Developers, administrators, and end-

users should be educated about the risks associated with session management and the best practices for secure usage. Implementing strict security policies and procedures, including session management guidelines, can help ensure that all stakeholders are aware of their responsibilities in maintaining session security. Finally, organizations should stay informed about the latest security threats and vulnerabilities by actively monitoring security advisories, participating in security communities, and sharing knowledge among their teams. In summary, session management vulnerabilities pose significant risks to web applications and user data. Session fixation, session hijacking, session timeout manipulation, and CSRF attacks can compromise user sessions and lead to security breaches. Safeguards, such as generating unique session IDs, using secure transport protocols, employing anti-CSRF tokens, and implementing data integrity checks, are essential to protect against these threats. Regular security testing, education, and awareness are critical components of a comprehensive strategy to mitigate session management vulnerabilities and maintain the security of web applications.

Chapter 7: Security Misconfigurations and Best Practices

Security misconfigurations are among the most prevalent and critical vulnerabilities in web applications, and they can have severe consequences if left unaddressed. These misconfigurations occur when web applications, servers, or databases are not set up securely, inadvertently exposing sensitive data and functionalities to attackers. Identifying and rectifying common security misconfigurations is essential for maintaining the integrity and confidentiality of web applications. One common security misconfiguration is leaving default credentials or passwords in place. Many web applications, databases, and servers come with default usernames and passwords that are well-known to attackers. Failure to change these default credentials creates a significant vulnerability, as attackers can easily gain unauthorized access to the system. To mitigate this risk, administrators should always change default credentials to strong, unique passwords during the initial setup. Another prevalent misconfiguration is overly permissive file or directory permissions. When web servers or applications have overly lax permissions, it becomes possible for attackers to view, modify, or delete critical files and data. Securing file and directory permissions by restricting access to authorized users and processes is crucial. Web application security scanners can help identify and remediate these issues by performing automated checks for insecure permissions.

Improper error handling is another frequent misconfiguration. When error messages reveal sensitive information, such as stack traces or database error details, attackers can exploit this information to identify vulnerabilities and potential attack vectors. Implementing custom error pages and ensuring that error messages do not disclose sensitive data is essential. Directory listing, also known as directory traversal or path disclosure, is a security misconfiguration that can expose the internal structure of a web application. Attackers can use this information to identify potentially vulnerable files and directories. Disabling directory listing in web server configurations is an effective measure to prevent this type of exposure. Insecure configuration of security headers is a critical misconfiguration. Security headers, such as HTTP Strict Transport Security (HSTS) and Cross-Origin Resource Sharing (CORS), can provide significant protection against various web vulnerabilities. However, misconfiguring these headers can weaken security. It's essential to configure security headers correctly to enhance protection against common attacks like cross-site scripting (XSS) and cross-site request forgery (CSRF). Unnecessary services or features that are enabled by default can also lead to security misconfigurations. Every service or feature enabled on a server or within an application potentially increases the attack surface. To minimize risks, administrators should disable or remove services and features that are not needed for the application's functionality. Failure to keep software and libraries up to date is a security misconfiguration that *can expose vulnerabilities. Outdated software may have known security issues that attackers can exploit. Regularly applying patches and updates to all components of a web application stack is essential to address these vulnerabilities. Insecure default settings in web applications or web server configurations are a significant source of security misconfigurations. Developers and administrators should review default settings and modify them as necessary to align with security best practices. A common misconfiguration involves allowing unrestricted file uploads in web applications. Attackers can upload malicious files, such as scripts or malware, which can be executed on the server. Implementing strict controls on file uploads, including file type validation and proper sanitization, can mitigate this risk. Inadequate logging and monitoring practices can lead to security misconfigurations. Without robust logging and monitoring, administrators may not detect and respond to security incidents promptly. Implementing comprehensive logging and continuous monitoring of system and application logs is crucial for identifying and addressing security issues. Improperly configured access controls are a significant source of security misconfigurations. Misconfigured access controls can lead to unauthorized access to sensitive data or functionality. Implementing strong access control measures, such as role-based access control (RBAC) and least privilege principles, is essential. Lack of proper security headers can expose web applications to security risks. Headers like Content Security Policy (CSP) and X-*

Content-Type-Options can protect against various attacks, including XSS and clickjacking. Configuring these headers correctly is crucial for enhancing web application security. Failure to use strong encryption for data in transit can result in security misconfigurations. Implementing protocols like HTTPS with the appropriate certificates is essential to protect data during transmission. Weak or non-existent authentication mechanisms are a common source of security misconfigurations. Web applications should enforce strong password policies, implement multi-factor authentication (MFA), and use secure authentication protocols like OAuth or SAML when applicable. Misconfigured security groups and firewall rules in cloud environments can expose sensitive resources to the internet. Administrators should review and tighten security group and firewall rule configurations to limit exposure and follow the principle of least privilege. The misconfiguration of security headers, such as Content Security Policy (CSP) or Cross-Origin Resource Sharing (CORS), can weaken a web application's defense against various web-based attacks. Developers should carefully configure these headers to ensure they provide the desired level of protection. In summary, security misconfigurations are common and can pose significant risks to web applications. Identifying and remediating these misconfigurations requires a proactive approach that includes regular security assessments, thorough testing, and adherence to security best practices. By addressing these vulnerabilities, organizations can enhance the security of their web applications and *protect sensitive data from potential breaches and attacks. Configuring web applications securely is a fundamental aspect of web application security, as misconfigurations can lead to vulnerabilities and potential data breaches. Proper configuration ensures that web applications operate as intended while safeguarding sensitive data, protecting against attacks, and minimizing the attack surface. One of the first steps in configuring a web application securely is to ensure that all software components, including the web server, application server, and database server, are up to date. Running outdated software can expose known vulnerabilities that attackers can exploit, so it's crucial to regularly apply patches and updates. Another essential aspect of secure configuration is the proper management of access controls. Access control lists (ACLs) should be carefully configured to restrict access to authorized users and roles, following the principle of least privilege. Unnecessary privileges should be revoked, and users should only have access to the resources necessary for their tasks. It's also important to implement strong authentication mechanisms to ensure that only authenticated and authorized users can access the application. This includes enforcing strong password policies, implementing multi-factor authentication (MFA), and using secure authentication protocols like OAuth or SAML when applicable. Secure configuration also involves setting up and configuring secure communication protocols, such as HTTPS. HTTPS encrypts data in transit, protecting it from eavesdropping and man-in-the-middle attacks. SSL/TLS* certificates should be properly installed and configured to ensure the security of data exchanged between the client and the server. Sensitive information, such as passwords and personal data, should never be transmitted in plain text. Web applications should use secure protocols and encryption for all communication. Configuring security headers correctly is another vital aspect of secure web application configuration. Security headers like Content Security Policy (CSP) and X-Content-Type-Options can provide significant protection against various web-based attacks. These headers should be carefully crafted to restrict potentially dangerous actions and protect against cross-site scripting (XSS) and other threats. To further enhance security, web applications should implement rate limiting and resource throttling. These measures can prevent abuse and mitigate the impact of denial-of-service (DoS) attacks. Configuring proper logging and monitoring is crucial for detecting and responding to security incidents. Comprehensive logs should be generated and monitored regularly to identify any unusual or suspicious activities. Logs can provide valuable insights into security events and help administrators respond promptly to potential threats. It's also important to configure intrusion detection and prevention systems (IDS/IPS) to enhance the security of web applications. These systems can identify and block malicious traffic, including known attack patterns and signatures. Secure configuration extends to the protection of sensitive files and directories. File permissions should be configured to restrict access to *authorized users and processes. By setting permissions appropriately, web applications can prevent unauthorized access, modification, or deletion of critical files and data. Regularly reviewing and updating these permissions is essential to maintain security. Error handling is another area where secure configuration plays a critical role. Error messages should not disclose sensitive information, such as stack traces or database error details, as this information can be exploited by attackers. Custom error pages should be implemented to handle errors gracefully and provide minimal information to users. Web application firewalls (WAFs) can be a valuable addition to the security stack, as they can help protect against a wide range of web-based attacks. Configuring and fine-tuning the WAF to filter and block malicious traffic is essential for effective security. Database configuration is a critical component of web application security. Database management systems should be configured securely to prevent unauthorized access and SQL injection attacks. Implementing parameterized queries and input validation can help mitigate the risk of SQL injection. Finally, secure configuration should be an ongoing process. Regular security assessments, vulnerability scanning, and penetration testing should be conducted to identify and remediate security issues. Security configurations should be reviewed and updated as the application evolves and new threats emerge. Security patches and updates should be applied promptly to address known vulnerabilities. In summary, configuring web applications securely is essential for protecting* against a wide range of security threats and vulnerabilities. From keeping software components up to date to implementing access controls, encryption, and secure communication protocols, there are numerous considerations for ensuring the security of web applications. By following best practices and staying vigilant, organizations can reduce the risk of security breaches and provide a safer online experience for their users.

Chapter 8: Web Application Firewalls (WAFs) and Intrusion Detection

Deploying and configuring a web application firewall (WAF) is a crucial step in enhancing the security of web applications, protecting against a wide range of threats, and ensuring the confidentiality, integrity, and availability of data. A WAF acts as a security barrier between a web application and the internet, inspecting incoming traffic and filtering out malicious requests and attacks. Before deploying a WAF, it's essential to have a clear understanding of the web application's architecture, functionality, and potential security vulnerabilities. This understanding will help determine the appropriate deployment method and configuration settings for the WAF. One common deployment method for a WAF is the reverse proxy mode. In this mode, the WAF sits in front of the web application server and intercepts all incoming traffic. It acts as a gatekeeper, inspecting each request before passing it to the web application. The reverse proxy mode allows the WAF to block malicious traffic, filter out attacks, and provide an additional layer of security without modifying the web application's code. Another deployment method is the transparent or inline mode, where the WAF is placed directly in the network path between clients and the web application. In this mode, the WAF inspects traffic in real-time and can block malicious requests before they reach the web application server. The choice between reverse proxy and transparent mode depends on the specific requirements and constraints of the web application and network architecture. Once the deployment method is chosen, the next step is to configure the WAF to effectively protect the web application. This includes setting up security policies, defining rules, and configuring various security features. A fundamental aspect of WAF configuration is defining security policies. Security policies specify the rules and actions that the WAF should take when it encounters different types of traffic. Policies should be tailored to the specific needs and vulnerabilities of the web application. For example, a security policy may include rules to block SQL injection attempts, cross-site scripting (XSS) attacks, and other common threats. Additionally, security policies should be regularly reviewed and updated to adapt to evolving threats and vulnerabilities. In configuring the WAF, administrators need to create and manage rules that define the conditions under which the WAF should take specific actions. Rules can be based on various criteria, such as request parameters, HTTP headers, IP addresses, or user-agent strings. For example, a rule can be created to block all incoming requests that contain known malicious patterns or signatures. Fine-tuning rules and continuously monitoring their effectiveness is essential to strike the right balance between security and usability. WAFs often include features for rate limiting and resource throttling. These features help mitigate the impact of denial-of-service (DoS) attacks and brute force attacks by limiting the number of requests from a single source within a specified time frame. Configuring rate limiting *and resource throttling settings is critical to ensure that legitimate users are not inadvertently blocked while protecting the web application from abuse. Web application firewalls can provide protection against various web-based attacks, including cross-site scripting (XSS), SQL injection, remote file inclusion, and more. Each type of attack requires specific configuration settings and rules to block or mitigate. For example, to protect against XSS attacks, the WAF may need to inspect and sanitize input data, validate HTML content, and block potentially malicious scripts. Similarly, for SQL injection protection, the WAF should inspect and validate SQL queries to prevent unauthorized access to the database. In addition to rule-based security policies, WAFs often offer features like anomaly detection and behavioral analysis. These capabilities can identify and block traffic that deviates from the normal patterns of behavior, which can be indicative of attacks or anomalies. Configuring and fine-tuning these features is essential to reduce false positives and ensure accurate threat detection. Monitoring and logging are crucial aspects of WAF configuration. WAFs generate logs that contain valuable information about incoming traffic, detected threats, and actions taken. These logs should be regularly reviewed and analyzed to identify potential security incidents, patterns of attack, and areas where the WAF configuration may need adjustment. Integrating the WAF with a Security Information and Event Management (SIEM) system or a log analysis tool can help automate log analysis and alerting. Additionally, real-time monitoring and alerting* mechanisms should be configured to notify administrators of potential threats and suspicious activities as they occur. Regularly updating and maintaining the WAF is essential to ensure its effectiveness. Security threats and attack techniques evolve over time, so it's crucial to keep the WAF's rule sets, signatures, and security policies up to date. Most WAF vendors release regular updates and patches to address emerging threats. Automating the update process and subscribing to threat intelligence feeds can help ensure that the WAF remains current and effective in blocking the latest threats. Finally, documentation and documentation should be created and maintained for the WAF configuration. This documentation should include details about the deployed security policies, rules, configuration settings, and any customizations made to the WAF. Having comprehensive documentation ensures that administrators can quickly reference and understand the WAF's configuration, facilitating troubleshooting, auditing, and compliance efforts.

Chapter 9: API Security Testing

Intrusion detection and prevention systems (IDPS) play a crucial role in enhancing the security of web applications by monitoring and safeguarding against various threats and attacks. The deployment of an IDPS within a web application environment is a proactive security measure that can help organizations detect and respond to unauthorized activities and security incidents in real-time. Before implementing an IDPS for web applications, it is essential to conduct a thorough assessment of the organization's security needs and objectives. This assessment will help determine the appropriate IDPS deployment model, configuration, and monitoring strategies. One common deployment model for IDPS in web applications is the network-based IDPS. In this model, the IDPS is positioned at strategic points within the network infrastructure to analyze incoming and outgoing traffic. It inspects network packets and can detect suspicious patterns, signatures, or anomalies that may indicate an intrusion or attack. Another deployment model is the host-based IDPS, which is installed directly on the web server or application server. The host-based IDPS focuses on monitoring the activities and processes occurring on the host itself, providing insights into potential security issues specific to the server. Web application firewalls (WAFs) often include intrusion detection and prevention capabilities, making them a popular choice for organizations looking to protect their web applications comprehensively. Once the deployment model is selected, configuring the IDPS for web applications is a critical step. Configuration involves defining detection rules, signatures, and policies to identify and respond to specific threats. Detection rules can be based on known attack patterns, vulnerabilities, or behavioral anomalies. Signatures are predefined patterns or sequences of data that match known attack techniques. Policies specify the actions the IDPS should take when it identifies a potential threat or intrusion. Fine-tuning these rules, signatures, and policies is crucial to minimizing false positives while ensuring that genuine threats are detected. The IDPS should be configured to log and alert on detected incidents promptly. Alerts can be sent to security teams or administrators via email, SMS, or integration with a Security Information and Event Management (SIEM) system. Additionally, the IDPS should have the capability to block or mitigate threats automatically based on predefined policies. However, automated actions should be carefully configured to avoid disrupting legitimate traffic or services. Regularly updating the IDPS is essential to keep it effective against evolving threats. Vendors release updates, patches, and new threat signatures to address emerging vulnerabilities and attack techniques. Automating the update process and subscribing to threat intelligence feeds can help ensure that the IDPS remains current and capable of detecting the latest threats. Monitoring and analyzing alerts generated by the IDPS is a continuous process. Security teams should actively review and investigate alerts to determine their significance and take appropriate action. This may *involve identifying the source of the attack, assessing its impact, and applying necessary countermeasures. Collaboration between security and IT teams is crucial to ensure effective incident response. Correlating IDPS alerts with other security events and logs from various sources can provide a more comprehensive view of potential security incidents. Threat intelligence feeds, such as indicators of compromise (IoC), should be integrated into the IDPS to enhance its ability to detect new threats and suspicious activities. Tuning the IDPS to align with the specific security needs of the web application is essential. Customizing detection rules and policies based on the web application's architecture, functionality, and vulnerabilities is critical for accurate threat detection. For example, if a web application is known to be vulnerable to a particular type of attack, the IDPS can be configured with specific rules to detect and block that attack vector. Regularly reviewing and optimizing these custom configurations is essential as the web application evolves and new vulnerabilities are discovered. IDPS alerts should be categorized and prioritized based on their severity and potential impact. Not all alerts require the same level of attention, and resources should be allocated based on the perceived risk. High-severity alerts that indicate ongoing attacks or breaches should be addressed immediately, while lower-severity alerts can be investigated and mitigated as resources allow. Intrusion prevention capabilities, such as the ability to block malicious traffic or terminate suspicious sessions, should be utilized judiciously. Blocking too aggressively can inadvertently disrupt* legitimate traffic or services. Security teams should carefully assess the potential impact of taking action on an alert before implementing automated blocking measures. Regularly reviewing the performance and effectiveness of the IDPS is essential. This includes assessing its ability to detect and respond to threats, as well as evaluating the rate of false positives and false negatives. Performance metrics should be analyzed to identify any bottlenecks or areas where the IDPS may need additional resources or fine-tuning. Finally, documenting the IDPS configuration, policies, and incident response procedures is crucial for maintaining transparency and accountability. Documentation should be kept up to date and made accessible to relevant personnel within the organization. In summary, implementing an intrusion detection and prevention system for web applications is a critical security measure that can help organizations proactively detect and respond to security threats and intrusions. By carefully selecting the deployment model, configuring the IDPS, continuously monitoring and fine-tuning its performance, and collaborating effectively within the organization, security teams can enhance the overall security posture of their web applications and protect against a wide range of threats. Application Programming Interfaces (APIs) have become a fundamental building block of modern software development, enabling the seamless integration of various services, platforms, and applications. As APIs continue to gain prominence, it's essential to recognize the vulnerabilities and risks associated with their use and implementation. API security is a critical aspect of overall cybersecurity, and understanding the potential threats is crucial for protecting sensitive data and maintaining the integrity of systems. One of the primary API vulnerabilities is inadequate authentication and authorization. When APIs are not properly secured, unauthorized users or malicious actors can gain access to sensitive data or perform actions they shouldn't be allowed to. Effective authentication mechanisms, such as OAuth 2.0 or API keys, are essential to ensure that only authorized users and applications can interact with the API. Authorization mechanisms should be granular, allowing access only to specific resources or actions based on user roles and permissions. Another common vulnerability is lack of encryption in transit and at rest. API data transmitted over the network should be encrypted using protocols like HTTPS to prevent eavesdropping and data interception. Data at rest should also be protected using encryption to safeguard it from unauthorized access in storage. Failure to implement encryption can lead to data breaches and exposure of sensitive information. API endpoints that are not adequately rate-limited are susceptible to abuse through brute force or denial-of-service (DoS) attacks. Rate limiting should be enforced to restrict the number of requests from a single source within a specified time frame, preventing excessive traffic and potential API abuse. Insecure deserialization is another critical API vulnerability that can lead to code execution attacks. Malicious payloads can be crafted to exploit vulnerabilities in the deserialization process, allowing *attackers to execute arbitrary code on the server. Implementing proper input validation and using libraries with secure deserialization practices is essential to mitigate this risk. Inconsistent error handling in APIs can reveal sensitive information to attackers. Error messages should not disclose internal details about the API's infrastructure or the underlying database schema. Instead, generic error messages should be provided to users while detailed error logs are maintained for internal analysis. Lack of proper access control and session management can also lead to API vulnerabilities. Sensitive data, such as authentication tokens or session cookies, should be securely managed and protected. Implementing robust access control mechanisms ensures that users can access only the resources and data they are authorized to. Cross-Site Scripting (XSS) vulnerabilities can also affect APIs when they interact with web applications. APIs should sanitize and validate user inputs to prevent the injection of malicious scripts that can compromise user sessions or steal sensitive information. Security misconfigurations in API endpoints, servers, or cloud services can expose vulnerabilities. Regular security audits and vulnerability assessments are essential to identify and remediate misconfigurations that could be exploited by attackers. APIs should also implement proper logging and monitoring to detect and respond to security incidents promptly. Lack of API versioning and backward compatibility can create challenges when updating or modifying APIs. Developers should follow versioning best practices and provide backward compatibility for existing clients to ensure a smooth transition and prevent disruptions. API endpoints should have proper rate limits in place to protect against abuse and DoS attacks. Rate limits should be set based on the expected usage patterns and capacity of the API, and they should be enforced consistently. Data validation and input validation should be performed rigorously to prevent injection attacks, such as SQL injection or NoSQL injection. API endpoints should validate user inputs and reject any malicious or malformed data to ensure the integrity of the system. APIs should implement strong authentication mechanisms, including multi-factor authentication (MFA), to ensure that only authorized users can access sensitive data and perform actions. API keys and tokens should be securely generated, managed, and revoked when necessary to maintain access control. Regular security testing, including penetration testing and vulnerability scanning, should be conducted to identify and address potential weaknesses in the API. Security assessments should be performed by skilled professionals who can identify and mitigate security flaws. APIs should follow the principle of least privilege, ensuring that users and applications have access only to the minimum resources and actions required to perform their tasks. This reduces the attack surface and limits the potential impact of security breaches. APIs should implement robust and well-defined logging and monitoring practices. Logs should capture relevant security events, and monitoring systems should alert administrators to any suspicious or anomalous activities. Incident response plans should be* in place to address security breaches or incidents promptly and effectively. This includes clear procedures for notifying affected parties and implementing remediation measures. API documentation should include comprehensive security guidelines and best practices for developers and users. Educating developers on secure API development and usage is crucial for maintaining a strong security posture. In summary, API vulnerabilities and risks are significant concerns in modern software development and cybersecurity. Addressing these vulnerabilities requires a combination of secure coding practices, robust authentication and authorization mechanisms, thorough testing, and ongoing monitoring. By proactively addressing API security, organizations can protect their systems, data, and users from potential threats and breaches.

Chapter 10: Exploiting Advanced Web Application Vulnerabilities

Web applications are a vital part of the digital landscape, serving various functions such as e-commerce, social networking, and online banking. While they bring convenience and functionality to users, web applications also present attractive targets for attackers seeking to exploit vulnerabilities for financial gain, data theft, or disruption of services. As organizations bolster their security measures, attackers continually evolve their tactics to circumvent defenses and carry out advanced attacks on web applications. One common advanced attack is the injection of malicious code, such as SQL injection or Cross-Site Scripting (XSS), into user inputs or data fields. These attacks exploit poor input validation and can lead to data breaches, unauthorized access, or the execution of malicious scripts within the application. Attackers may use automated tools to identify and exploit vulnerable input points, making it crucial for developers to implement rigorous input validation and output encoding to prevent these attacks. Another advanced attack vector is XML External Entity (XXE) injection. This attack targets web applications that process XML input without proper validation, allowing attackers to read arbitrary files, perform remote reconnaissance, or launch denial-of-service attacks. To mitigate XXE attacks, developers should disable external entity processing or employ secure parsing libraries that prevent malicious entity expansion. Advanced attackers may also attempt to exploit server-side request forgery (SSRF) vulnerabilities. SSRF allows attackers to make HTTP requests from the server, potentially accessing internal resources, bypassing security controls, or launching attacks on other systems. To defend against SSRF, organizations should implement strong input validation, employ whitelisting of trusted resources, and restrict the application's ability to access external URLs. Furthermore, attackers frequently employ evasion techniques to bypass security mechanisms. For instance, they may use encoding or obfuscation to hide malicious payloads from detection by web application firewalls (WAFs) or intrusion detection systems (IDS). Developers should be aware of these tactics and regularly update security controls to detect and mitigate evasive attacks. A less well-known but increasingly prevalent attack is deserialization attacks. Attackers manipulate serialized objects sent to a web application, leading to remote code execution or unauthorized access. Developers should use secure deserialization libraries, validate serialized objects, and restrict access to deserialization endpoints to prevent such attacks. Credential stuffing is a pervasive advanced attack that leverages reused or stolen usernames and passwords across multiple websites. Attackers use automated tools to test compromised credentials against various web applications, exploiting users who reuse passwords and potentially gaining unauthorized access. To defend against credential stuffing, organizations should enforce strong password policies, implement multi-factor authentication (MFA), and monitor for unusual login activity. Moreover, attackers may conduct distributed denial-of-service (DDoS) attacks to overwhelm web application servers and disrupt services. Advanced attackers may utilize botnets, amplification techniques, or application-layer attacks to bypass traditional DDoS mitigation measures. Organizations should implement robust DDoS protection solutions and incident response plans to mitigate the impact of DDoS attacks on web applications. Intrusion attempts and account takeovers are also common advanced attacks. Attackers may employ brute force, credential stuffing, or social engineering to compromise user accounts, gaining unauthorized access or performing malicious actions. To counter these attacks, organizations should implement account lockout mechanisms, rate limiting, and strong authentication methods. Moreover, web application security must extend beyond the application layer to include secure server and database configurations. Insecure server settings or misconfigured databases can expose sensitive data or provide attackers with unintended access. Developers should follow security best practices, regularly patch and update servers and databases, and limit access to essential personnel. Furthermore, advanced attacks may exploit application vulnerabilities to gain access to underlying operating systems. This can result in full server compromise, allowing attackers to execute arbitrary code, pivot to other systems, or install backdoors. Security assessments, vulnerability scanning, and regular patch management are essential to prevent these attacks. Advanced attackers may also target third-party *components or dependencies used in web applications. Vulnerabilities in third-party libraries, frameworks, or plugins can serve as entry points for attackers. Organizations should track and update third-party components regularly and subscribe to vulnerability feeds to stay informed about security patches. In addition to technical measures, organizations must prioritize security awareness and training. Employees, including developers and users, should be educated about common threats and best practices to recognize and respond to security incidents. Attackers often employ social engineering techniques, such as phishing, to trick users into revealing sensitive information or executing malicious actions. User awareness and vigilance are crucial defenses against such attacks. Lastly, continuous monitoring and incident response capabilities are essential to detect, respond to, and recover from advanced attacks on web applications. Security teams should have the tools and processes in place to identify anomalous behavior, investigate security incidents, and contain and mitigate threats promptly. Regularly conducting security audits, penetration testing, and threat modeling can help organizations proactively identify and address vulnerabilities before attackers exploit them. In summary, advanced attacks on web applications are a persistent and evolving threat. Organizations must remain vigilant, employ a layered security approach, and stay informed about emerging attack techniques. By prioritizing security at every stage of development and deployment, organizations can reduce the risk of falling victim to advanced web application attacks and protect their users and data from harm. To gain a deeper understanding of web application vulnerabilities and their real-world implications, let's explore several noteworthy examples of successful exploitation. One prominent vulnerability is SQL injection, which allows attackers to manipulate a web application's database. In 2017, the Equifax data breach exposed sensitive data of 147 million people due to an unpatched SQL injection vulnerability. Attackers exploited this vulnerability to exfiltrate personal and financial information, highlighting the devastating consequences of such flaws. Another prevalent vulnerability is Cross-Site Scripting (XSS), which enables attackers to inject malicious scripts into web pages viewed by other users. In 2013, the Syrian Electronic Army used XSS attacks to compromise high-profile media websites like The New York Times and Twitter. They injected propaganda messages and disrupted services, demonstrating the impact of XSS in the real world. Insecure authentication mechanisms can also lead to severe consequences. In 2014, the Heartbleed vulnerability exposed a flaw in OpenSSL, a widely-used cryptographic library. Attackers could steal sensitive data, including login credentials, from vulnerable websites. This vulnerability affected numerous organizations, underscoring the importance of robust authentication measures. Web application misconfigurations are another common issue. In 2019, Capital One suffered a data breach due to a misconfigured web application firewall (WAF). The attacker exploited the misconfiguration to access* sensitive customer data, emphasizing the need for proper configuration management. Insufficient access controls can have dire consequences as well. In 2019, a WhatsApp vulnerability allowed attackers to install spyware on users' phones without their consent. This breach showcased the importance of robust access controls in protecting user privacy. Session management vulnerabilities are also a concern. In 2013, a flaw in Apple's iCloud service allowed attackers to reset user passwords and gain unauthorized access to accounts. Apple quickly addressed the issue, but it serves as a reminder of the critical role of secure session management. Inadequate input validation can lead to devastating attacks. In 2018, a vulnerability in a popular WordPress plugin, GDPR Cookie Consent, allowed attackers to inject malicious JavaScript code into websites. This resulted in user data theft and site defacement, emphasizing the importance of rigorous input validation. API vulnerabilities can impact web applications as well. In 2020, a security flaw in the OAuth 2.0 protocol led to unauthorized access to user accounts in the Shopify e-commerce platform. This incident highlighted the significance of secure API design and implementation. Web application firewalls (WAFs) are crucial for defense, but they can be bypassed. In 2021, researchers discovered that bypassing a WAF's ruleset was possible by encoding malicious payloads in innovative ways. This finding demonstrated the need for continuous WAF monitoring and rule refinement. Security researchers and ethical hackers play a vital role in uncovering vulnerabilities before malicious actors *exploit them. For example, in 2021, a researcher identified a vulnerability in a widely-used Log4j library, which could lead to remote code execution. Swift action was taken to address the issue, showcasing the importance of responsible disclosure. One of the most significant recent breaches occurred in 2021 when the Colonial Pipeline Company fell victim to a ransomware attack. Attackers exploited a vulnerability in the company's virtual private network (VPN) to gain unauthorized access. This incident disrupted fuel supplies across the Eastern United States, underscoring the potential societal impact of web application vulnerabilities. In summary, real-world examples of exploiting web application vulnerabilities demonstrate the critical importance of security measures in the digital age. Developers, security professionals, and organizations must remain vigilant, prioritize security, and proactively address vulnerabilities to protect users and data from the ever-evolving threat landscape.*

BOOK 4
PENTESTING 101
MASTERING CYBERSECURITY CHALLENGES AND BEYOND

ROB BOTWRIGHT

Chapter 1: Evolving Threat Landscape and Security Trends

In today's rapidly evolving cybersecurity landscape, understanding the threat actors and their tactics is crucial for defending against cyberattacks. Sophisticated threat actors, often associated with nation-states, employ advanced tactics, techniques, and procedures (TTPs) to achieve their objectives. These nation-state actors are motivated by geopolitical interests and engage in espionage, cyber-espionage, and sabotage to gain a competitive advantage or influence global affairs. One of the most notorious nation-state threat actors is APT29, also known as Cozy Bear, believed to be affiliated with the Russian government. APT29 is known for its sophisticated spear-phishing campaigns, zero-day exploits, and extensive use of custom malware to target government agencies, defense contractors, and critical infrastructure. Another prominent nation-state threat actor is APT28, also known as Fancy Bear, which is also linked to Russia. Fancy Bear is known for its involvement in high-profile cyberattacks, including the hacking of the Democratic National Committee (DNC) in 2016. It has a history of using phishing, malware, and disinformation campaigns to further its objectives. China is another nation-state actor with a robust cyber capability, and APT41 is one of its most active threat groups. APT41 is unique in that it engages in both state-sponsored cyber-espionage and financially motivated cybercrime. Their tactics include supply chain attacks, ransomware campaigns, and targeted espionage against a wide range of sectors. North Korea, through its Lazarus Group, conducts cyberattacks for both financial gain and political purposes. The Lazarus Group was responsible for the 2014 Sony Pictures hack and the 2017 WannaCry ransomware attack, among others. They employ spear-phishing, watering hole attacks, and cryptocurrency theft to fund the regime and circumvent international sanctions. Iran also has a history of cyberattacks, and APT33 is one of the Iranian threat groups. APT33 has targeted organizations in the aerospace, energy, and petrochemical industries, using spear-phishing and malware to compromise critical infrastructure. Non-nation-state threat actors, such as hacktivists, cybercriminals, and cyber mercenaries, are also active and pose significant challenges to cybersecurity. Hacktivist groups, like Anonymous, engage in cyberattacks to promote social or political causes. They often use distributed denial-of-service (DDoS) attacks, website defacement, and data leaks to achieve their goals. Cybercriminals operate with financial gain in mind and employ tactics such as phishing, ransomware, and identity theft to steal money or sensitive data. Ransomware attacks have become particularly prevalent, with groups like REvil, DarkSide, and Conti making headlines. These groups demand ransoms from victims in exchange for decrypting their data or not leaking stolen information. Cyber mercenaries are a unique and emerging threat actor category. They are private individuals or groups hired by governments or organizations to conduct cyberattacks on their behalf.

These mercenaries often have advanced technical skills and carry out targeted espionage or disruption campaigns. In addition to threat actors, understanding the tactics they employ is essential for effective cybersecurity. Phishing remains one of the most common tactics used by threat actors. Phishing emails attempt to trick recipients into revealing sensitive information or downloading malicious attachments. Spear-phishing takes this a step further by targeting specific individuals or organizations with tailored messages. Ransomware attacks have grown in frequency and sophistication, encrypting victims' data and demanding a ransom for its release. Some threat actors, like Ryuk and Maze, have adopted "double extortion" tactics, threatening to leak stolen data if the ransom is not paid. Supply chain attacks have become a significant concern, where attackers compromise trusted suppliers or software vendors to infiltrate their target organizations. Notable examples include the SolarWinds supply chain attack and the compromise of the software development tool, Codecov. Zero-day exploits are valuable tools for threat actors, as they target vulnerabilities that are unknown to the software vendor. These exploits can be used to gain initial access or escalate privileges within a target system. Watering hole attacks involve compromising websites frequently visited by the target audience. When users visit these compromised sites, malware is delivered to their devices. Advanced persistent threats (APTs) are characterized by stealthy, long-term campaigns, often associated with nation-state actors. They employ a *combination of tactics, including spear-phishing, custom malware, and lateral movement within compromised networks. Disinformation campaigns are used to spread false or misleading information for political, social, or economic purposes. These campaigns often exploit social media platforms and manipulate public opinion. Infiltration of critical infrastructure, such as power grids, water treatment plants, and healthcare systems, is a growing concern. Threat actors seek to disrupt these vital systems, potentially causing physical harm and economic damage. Fileless malware is a stealthy tactic where malicious code is executed directly in memory, leaving no trace on the victim's disk. This makes detection and forensic analysis challenging. Internet of Things (IoT) devices are increasingly targeted by threat actors, as they often lack robust security measures. Compromised IoT devices can be used to launch attacks or provide an entry point into larger networks. To mitigate these threats, organizations must adopt a proactive cybersecurity strategy. This includes implementing strong access controls, regularly patching software and systems, conducting security awareness training, and developing an incident response plan. Collaboration with government agencies, threat intelligence sharing, and engaging with cybersecurity experts are also essential components of a comprehensive defense strategy. In summary, the ever-evolving threat landscape presents a diverse range of threat actors and tactics. Understanding these adversaries and their methods is crucial for organizations and individuals alike to protect against* cyberattacks and safeguard sensitive data and critical systems. As technology continues to advance at a rapid pace, the world of cybersecurity faces a constantly shifting landscape filled with new trends and challenges. Next, we will explore some of the most prominent emerging security trends and the challenges they present to individuals, organizations, and society as a whole.

One of the foremost emerging trends in cybersecurity is the increasing sophistication of cyberattacks. Attackers are continually refining their tactics, techniques, and procedures to evade detection and infiltrate even the most well-defended networks. This escalation in sophistication has led to a rise in advanced persistent threats (APTs) and nation-state-sponsored attacks.

The use of artificial intelligence (AI) and machine learning (ML) in cyberattacks is another notable trend. Attackers are leveraging AI and ML to automate their attacks, identify vulnerabilities, and adapt their strategies in real-time. This not only makes attacks more efficient but also harder to detect.

On the defensive side, cybersecurity professionals are also turning to AI and ML to enhance threat detection and response. These technologies can analyze vast amounts of data to identify unusual patterns and potential threats. However, the challenge lies in staying ahead of attackers who are also harnessing AI for malicious purposes.

The Internet of Things (IoT) is expanding rapidly, with billions of interconnected devices now part of our daily lives. While IoT offers convenience and efficiency, it also *introduces significant security challenges. Many IoT devices have limited built-in security features, making them vulnerable to exploitation. Ensuring the security of IoT ecosystems remains a pressing concern.*

Another emerging trend is the convergence of IT (Information Technology) and OT (Operational Technology) in critical infrastructure. Industries like energy, manufacturing, and healthcare are integrating IT systems with traditionally isolated OT networks. This convergence increases efficiency but exposes critical infrastructure to new cyber risks, such as ransomware attacks targeting industrial control systems.

Cloud computing has become the backbone of modern business operations, offering scalability and flexibility. However, securing cloud environments and data stored there is a complex challenge. Misconfigurations, unauthorized access, and data breaches in the cloud pose significant threats.

Zero-trust security models are gaining traction as organizations shift away from the traditional perimeter-based approach. Zero-trust assumes that threats may already exist inside the network and requires strict identity verification and access controls for all users and devices. Implementing this model can be a daunting task for large organizations with complex networks.

The rise of remote work and the continued adoption of hybrid work models bring new security concerns. Employees accessing corporate networks and sensitive data from various locations and devices create additional attack vectors. Balancing the need for flexibility with robust security measures is an ongoing challenge.

Privacy concerns are also growing, fueled by increased data collection, surveillance, and the monetization of personal information by technology companies. Data breaches and mishandling of personal data erode trust and raise questions about the adequacy of privacy regulations and enforcement.

Cybersecurity workforce shortages are a persistent challenge. The demand for skilled cybersecurity professionals far exceeds the supply. Closing this talent gap requires concerted efforts in education, training, and industry collaboration.

Supply chain attacks are garnering attention due to their potential for widespread impact. Attackers compromise trusted suppliers or software vendors to infiltrate their target organizations. Strengthening supply chain security and vetting third-party vendors have become critical.

The need for international cooperation in cybersecurity has never been more apparent. Many cyber threats transcend borders, making it essential for nations to work together to deter malicious actors, share threat intelligence, and establish norms for responsible behavior in cyberspace.

While technological advancements bring both benefits and risks, the human element remains a constant factor in cybersecurity. Social engineering attacks, such as phishing and spear-phishing, continue to exploit human psychology and trust. Educating individuals about these tactics and promoting cybersecurity awareness is vital.

The legal and regulatory landscape in cybersecurity is evolving as governments seek to address emerging threats. Data protection regulations like the General Data Protection Regulation (GDPR) in Europe and the California Consumer Privacy Act (CCPA) in the United States are examples of efforts to protect individuals' privacy and hold organizations accountable for data breaches.

Cybersecurity insurance is another developing trend. Organizations are increasingly seeking insurance coverage to mitigate the financial impact of cyber incidents. However, the assessment of cyber risks and the determination of insurance premiums remain challenging.

The intersection of cybersecurity and ethics is a growing concern. Ethical considerations around the use of hacking tools, the conduct of penetration testing, and the responsibilities of cybersecurity professionals are gaining attention. Ensuring that cybersecurity practices align with ethical principles is essential.

In summary, the evolving cybersecurity landscape presents a multitude of challenges and opportunities. As technology advances, so do the threats, requiring constant vigilance, innovation, and collaboration. Addressing these emerging trends and challenges is essential to safeguarding our digital world and the privacy and security of individuals and organizations alike.

Chapter 2: Advanced Attack Vectors and Techniques

Zero-day vulnerabilities are one of the most enigmatic and dangerous aspects of cybersecurity. These vulnerabilities, often shrouded in secrecy, pose a significant threat to individuals, organizations, and even governments. Next, we will delve into the world of zero-day vulnerabilities and exploits, exploring what they are, how they work, and the challenges they present in the realm of cybersecurity.

A zero-day vulnerability is a software flaw or weakness that is unknown to the vendor or developer. Unlike known vulnerabilities, which have been discovered and often patched, zero-day vulnerabilities have not yet been identified or addressed. This gives attackers a unique advantage because they can exploit these vulnerabilities without fear of immediate detection or mitigation.

The term "zero-day" refers to the fact that there are zero days of protection against these vulnerabilities when they are first discovered and exploited. It's as if the clock starts ticking on the day the vulnerability is disclosed or used in an attack. Zero-day vulnerabilities are highly coveted by cybercriminals, nation-state actors, and security researchers alike.

The process of discovering and exploiting a zero-day vulnerability typically follows a clandestine path. It often begins with a skilled individual or group of researchers seeking out vulnerabilities in software, operating systems, or applications. These researchers are often referred to as "white hat" hackers or security experts who aim to identify and responsibly disclose vulnerabilities to the affected vendors.

Once a zero-day vulnerability is found, the next step is crafting an exploit. An exploit is a piece of code or a technique that takes advantage of the vulnerability to gain unauthorized access, control, or privilege escalation within a targeted system or application. Exploits can vary in complexity, from simple scripts to highly sophisticated attack vectors.

The value of zero-day vulnerabilities and their corresponding exploits is significant. Cybercriminals can use them to breach systems, steal sensitive data, deploy malware, or launch attacks with devastating consequences. Nation-state actors may employ zero-day exploits for espionage, sabotage, or cyber warfare, giving them a strategic advantage on the global stage.

The underground market for zero-day vulnerabilities and exploits is a clandestine world where both buyers and sellers operate discreetly. Cybercriminals and governments are willing to pay substantial sums for these tools and knowledge. Prices for zero-day exploits can range from thousands to millions of dollars, depending on factors like the target software, the potential impact, and the level of secrecy surrounding the exploit.

One of the primary challenges in dealing with zero-day vulnerabilities is the lack of advanced warning or security patches. When a zero-day vulnerability is exploited, defenders are caught off guard, and there is no immediate solution provided by the software vendor. This "zero-day window" is the period during which organizations and individuals are vulnerable to attacks.

To protect against zero-day vulnerabilities, organizations must adopt a proactive and multi-layered cybersecurity strategy. This includes regularly updating software and *systems, implementing strong access controls, monitoring network traffic for unusual patterns, and conducting vulnerability assessments and penetration testing.*

Security researchers and ethical hackers also play a critical role in identifying and reporting zero-day vulnerabilities. Responsible disclosure is the process of privately informing the vendor about a vulnerability, allowing them time to develop and release a patch before the vulnerability is publicly disclosed. This responsible approach helps protect users while giving vendors an opportunity to address the issue.

Zero-day vulnerabilities highlight the ongoing cat-and-mouse game between attackers and defenders in the cybersecurity arena. As defenders work to fortify systems and discover vulnerabilities before attackers, malicious actors continuously seek new zero-day opportunities to exploit. This dynamic landscape underscores the need for constant vigilance, innovation, and collaboration within the cybersecurity community.

In summary, zero-day vulnerabilities and exploits are powerful weapons in the hands of cybercriminals and state-sponsored actors. Their ability to evade detection and mitigation makes them a persistent and formidable threat. Organizations and individuals must remain vigilant, proactive, and informed to defend against the unknown vulnerabilities that may lurk in the digital shadows.

Chapter 3: Post-Exploitation and Privilege Escalation

In the world of cybersecurity, the concept of "maintaining access after compromise" is a critical and often covert aspect of cyberattacks. When an attacker successfully infiltrates a system or network, they aim not only to gain initial access but also to maintain a persistent presence. Next, we will explore the tactics, techniques, and procedures used by attackers to achieve and sustain this persistent access, as well as the defensive strategies organizations can employ to detect and mitigate such threats.

The first step in maintaining access after compromise involves establishing a foothold within the target environment. Attackers frequently use various methods to achieve this, such as exploiting vulnerabilities, leveraging stolen credentials, or using malware to create backdoors. Once inside, they seek ways to ensure their continued presence, even if their initial point of entry is discovered and closed.

One common method used by attackers to maintain access is the installation of rootkits or backdoors. A rootkit is a set of malicious tools and code that allows an attacker to gain privileged access to a compromised system. It can modify system files and configurations to conceal its presence and maintain control over the compromised machine. Backdoors, on the other hand, provide a hidden entry point that allows an attacker to access the system at a later time, bypassing authentication mechanisms.

Another technique employed by attackers is privilege escalation. By exploiting vulnerabilities or misconfigurations, they can elevate their privileges to gain administrative or higher-level access within the target environment. Privilege escalation enables attackers to perform more significant actions, such as creating additional user accounts, modifying security settings, or exfiltrating sensitive data.

Persistence mechanisms are crucial for attackers seeking to maintain access. These mechanisms are designed to ensure that their malicious activities continue even after system reboots or security updates. Common persistence mechanisms include adding registry entries, scheduling tasks, modifying startup configurations, and employing rootkit technology.

Remote access tools (RATs) are often used by attackers to maintain control over compromised systems. RATs enable remote administration of a compromised device, allowing the attacker to execute commands, exfiltrate data, and interact with the system from a distance. Popular RATs include Metasploit's Meterpreter, Poison Ivy, and Gh0st RAT.

Command and control (C2) infrastructure is a critical component of maintaining access. Attackers set up C2 servers or channels to communicate with compromised systems. These channels facilitate the exchange of commands, updates, and stolen data between the attacker and the compromised devices. Detecting and disrupting C2 communication is a key defense strategy.

Data exfiltration is another goal for attackers maintaining access. They aim to steal sensitive information, intellectual property, or valuable data from the compromised environment. Attackers use various techniques, such as encrypting stolen data, disguising it within seemingly innocent traffic, or staging it for later retrieval.

Attackers must also evade detection during their persistence efforts. To achieve this, they employ anti-forensic techniques, which involve erasing or altering traces of their presence. This may include deleting logs, modifying timestamps, and obfuscating file attributes to make their activities less conspicuous.

Defenders must employ a multi-faceted approach to detect and mitigate attackers attempting to maintain access. Continuous monitoring and threat detection tools can help identify unusual or suspicious behavior within the network. Anomalies in network traffic, system activities, or user behavior can be indicators of compromise.

Incident response plans are essential for organizations to respond effectively when a persistent attacker is detected. These plans outline the steps to take when an intrusion is confirmed, including isolating compromised systems, collecting evidence, and removing malicious code.

Implementing strong access controls, proper patch management, and least privilege principles can help prevent privilege escalation and unauthorized access. Regular security audits and penetration testing can also identify vulnerabilities that attackers might exploit.

Network segmentation is a valuable defensive strategy that limits an attacker's lateral movement within a network. By dividing the network into isolated segments, organizations can contain and minimize the impact of a compromise.

Endpoint detection and response (EDR) solutions provide real-time visibility into endpoint activities and help detect and respond to malicious behavior. They can also aid in the investigation of incidents and the removal of persistent threats.

In summary, maintaining access after compromise is a critical phase in cyberattacks, and attackers employ various tactics and techniques to achieve this goal. Organizations must be proactive in their defense, implementing robust security measures, monitoring for suspicious activity, and having incident response plans in place. By understanding the tactics used by attackers and implementing effective countermeasures, organizations can reduce the risk of persistent threats and protect their valuable data and systems.

Privilege escalation is a critical concept in the field of cybersecurity, referring to the process by which an attacker gains higher levels of access and control within a system or network than originally granted. This chapter explores privilege escalation techniques and strategies, shedding light on how attackers exploit vulnerabilities and weaknesses to elevate their privileges, and how defenders can counter these threats.

Privilege escalation can take various forms, depending on the attacker's goals and the specific vulnerabilities or misconfigurations present. One common type is local privilege escalation, where an attacker with limited access on a system seeks to gain administrative or root-level privileges. This can be achieved through the exploitation of vulnerabilities in the operating system or applications running on the target system.

For example, attackers may search for software vulnerabilities that allow them to execute arbitrary code with higher privileges, exploiting vulnerabilities like buffer overflows, race conditions, or insecure file permissions to escalate their access. These vulnerabilities can be found in both the operating system and third-party applications, making regular patching and updates crucial for defense.

Kernel-level privilege escalation is a particularly powerful form of local privilege escalation, as it provides attackers with control over the core of the operating system. To achieve this, attackers may target kernel vulnerabilities or misconfigured kernel modules, enabling them to execute code at the highest privilege level.

Another avenue for privilege escalation is through the abuse of weak or misconfigured user accounts and permissions. Attackers may attempt to manipulate user roles, escalate their privileges, or impersonate other users with higher privileges by exploiting misconfigurations in access control mechanisms. This can include exploiting overly permissive file permissions, inadequate password policies, or weak authentication mechanisms.

Web application privilege escalation is a specific area of concern, where attackers seek to exploit vulnerabilities in web applications to gain unauthorized access to sensitive functions or data. This may involve *manipulating session variables, bypassing authorization controls, or exploiting application logic flaws.*

Network privilege escalation occurs when attackers attempt to move laterally within a network, escalating their privileges to gain control over additional systems or resources. This can involve exploiting vulnerabilities in network protocols, leveraging compromised credentials, or taking advantage of misconfigured access control lists (ACLs).

While attackers have a range of techniques at their disposal, defenders can employ several strategies to detect and mitigate privilege escalation threats. Regularly applying security patches and updates is a fundamental practice that helps eliminate known vulnerabilities that attackers may exploit for privilege escalation.

Monitoring and auditing user account activities can help identify suspicious behavior indicative of privilege escalation attempts. Anomalous login patterns, repeated failed authentication attempts, or sudden changes in user permissions can all be red flags.

Implementing the principle of least privilege (PoLP) is a proactive strategy to limit the potential impact of privilege escalation. By granting users and processes only the minimum level of access required to perform their tasks, organizations can reduce the attack surface and limit the potential for unauthorized escalation.

Network segmentation is a defensive strategy that can help contain the lateral movement of attackers within a network. By dividing the network into isolated segments with restricted communication paths, organizations can prevent attackers from easily escalating their privileges across the entire network.

Endpoint detection and response (EDR) solutions provide real-time visibility into endpoint activities and can help detect and respond to privilege escalation attempts. These solutions can also aid in the investigation of incidents and the removal of persistent threats.

Regular penetration testing and red team exercises can help organizations identify vulnerabilities and weaknesses that attackers may exploit for privilege escalation. By simulating real-world attack scenarios, organizations can proactively address and remediate these issues.

In summary, privilege escalation is a significant cybersecurity concern, and attackers employ various techniques to elevate their access and control within systems and networks. Defenders must adopt a multi-faceted approach that includes regular patching, user account monitoring, least privilege principles, network segmentation, and the use of security tools to detect and respond to privilege escalation attempts. By understanding the tactics used by attackers and implementing robust countermeasures, organizations can enhance their security posture and mitigate the risks associated with privilege escalation.

Chapter 4: Advanced Network Analysis and Packet Crafting

Deep Packet Inspection (DPI) is a sophisticated network monitoring and analysis technique that allows for in-depth examination of the contents of data packets traversing a network. Next, we will explore the concept of DPI, its applications, and the tools and strategies used to perform deep packet inspection and analysis effectively.

At its core, DPI involves the examination of individual data packets that make up network traffic, including their headers and payload content. This level of scrutiny enables network administrators, security professionals, and researchers to gain valuable insights into network activities and potential security threats.

One of the primary applications of DPI is network traffic monitoring and analysis. By inspecting packets in real-time, organizations can gain a comprehensive view of the traffic patterns within their networks. DPI can reveal the source and destination of packets, the protocols being used, and the types of data being transmitted.

Deep packet inspection also plays a crucial role in network security. It allows for the detection of malicious activities and threats by analyzing packet contents for signs of intrusion attempts, malware, or suspicious behavior. Security appliances and intrusion detection systems (IDS) often use DPI to identify and block potential threats.

To perform deep packet inspection and analysis effectively, several key components and techniques are employed. Packet capture tools, such as Wireshark and tcpdump, are essential for capturing network traffic and storing it for later analysis. These tools enable network administrators to record packets as they pass through network interfaces.

Once packets are captured, they can be analyzed using various software solutions designed for deep packet inspection. These tools offer features like protocol analysis, traffic filtering, and the ability to create custom rules to detect specific patterns or signatures indicative of security threats.

Signature-based detection is a common approach in DPI for identifying known threats. Security software uses predefined signatures or patterns to recognize and flag packets or traffic flows that match known attack patterns. This method is effective against well-known threats but may struggle with zero-day attacks or previously unseen threats.

Behavioral analysis is another DPI technique that focuses on monitoring network activities for unusual or suspicious behavior. Instead of relying on predefined signatures, behavioral analysis looks for deviations from established baselines. This approach is more adaptable to detecting new or evolving threats.

Encrypted traffic presents a challenge for DPI since it obscures the payload content of packets. However, some DPI solutions can perform decryption and inspection of encrypted traffic, known as SSL/TLS inspection. This process involves intercepting and *decrypting encrypted traffic flows to analyze their contents for security threats.*

Packet filtering and traffic shaping are additional DPI capabilities used to control network traffic. Packet filtering allows organizations to define rules for permitting or blocking specific types of traffic based on criteria such as source IP address, destination port, or protocol. Traffic shaping, on the other hand, prioritizes or limits the bandwidth of specific traffic types to optimize network performance.

When implementing DPI, organizations must consider privacy and compliance concerns, as deep packet inspection can potentially capture sensitive or personal data. To address these concerns, organizations should adhere to privacy regulations, inform users of monitoring activities, and implement data anonymization or encryption when necessary.

In summary, deep packet inspection and analysis are valuable tools in network management and security. By examining the contents of data packets, organizations can gain insights into network activities, detect security threats, and optimize network performance. However, the implementation of DPI must be done carefully to balance security needs with privacy and compliance requirements. With the right tools and techniques, DPI can be a powerful asset in the arsenal of network administrators and security professionals.

Chapter 5: Advanced Web Application Penetration Testing

Web applications have become a cornerstone of modern business operations, serving as the interface between users and valuable data. However, this increased reliance on web applications has also made them a prime target for cyberattacks. Next, we delve into advanced techniques for web application security testing, equipping you with the knowledge and tools to identify vulnerabilities, assess risks, and ensure the robustness of your web applications.

When it comes to web application security testing, there are several essential methodologies that every security professional should be familiar with. These methodologies provide a structured approach to uncovering vulnerabilities and assessing the security posture of web applications. One widely recognized methodology is the Open Web Application Security Project (OWASP) Top Ten, which lists common web application vulnerabilities such as injection attacks, broken authentication, and insecure direct object references.

Another crucial methodology is the Web Application Security Testing (WAST) methodology, which provides a comprehensive framework for testing web applications. WAST covers areas like information gathering, configuration management, authentication, and session management testing, and it offers detailed guidance on the testing process.

To conduct effective web application security testing, you need a diverse set of tools and techniques at your disposal. Automated vulnerability scanners are valuable assets for quickly identifying common vulnerabilities such as SQL injection and cross-site scripting (XSS). Tools like Burp Suite and OWASP ZAP can automate many aspects of web application testing, from spidering to fuzzing to reporting.

Manual testing is equally essential, as it allows testers to go beyond the capabilities of automated scanners and identify unique vulnerabilities. Manual testing involves carefully crafting input and monitoring the application's responses, looking for any signs of abnormal behavior or security weaknesses. This approach can uncover vulnerabilities like business logic flaws and access control issues that automated scanners may miss.

During web application security testing, it's crucial to assess the effectiveness of authentication and session management mechanisms. This includes testing for weak password policies, password recovery mechanisms, and ensuring that session tokens are adequately protected against theft or manipulation. Techniques like session fixation and session hijacking testing help identify weaknesses in session management.

Testing for security misconfigurations is another critical aspect of web application security testing. Security misconfigurations can expose sensitive information or provide attackers with unintended access. Reviewing application and server configurations, examining error messages, and ensuring that default credentials are changed are all part of this process.

Cross-Site Scripting (XSS) attacks continue to be a prevalent threat in web applications. Advanced XSS testing techniques include exploring different contexts where XSS can occur, such as in HTML, JavaScript, and various HTML attributes. Testing for DOM-based XSS, where client-side scripts manipulate the Document Object Model, is also essential.

Another critical area of focus in web application security testing is input validation and sanitization. Testers should thoroughly assess how the application handles user input, checking for vulnerabilities like SQL injection, command injection, and LDAP injection. Testing various encodings and payloads helps identify potential weaknesses.

Web application firewalls (WAFs) are often used to protect web applications from attacks. Advanced testing techniques involve bypassing WAF filters to discover vulnerabilities that may be obscured by the firewall. Techniques like encoding and obfuscation can be used to evade detection by WAFs.

Web services, such as REST and SOAP APIs, are integral components of many web applications. Testing these APIs for security vulnerabilities, including authentication flaws, authorization issues, and input validation, is crucial. Tools like Postman and SoapUI can assist in API testing.

To enhance your web application security testing skills, it's essential to stay updated on the latest attack techniques and emerging vulnerabilities. Following security blogs, attending conferences, and participating in capture the flag (CTF) competitions can help you hone your skills and learn from experienced professionals.

In summary, web application security testing is a critical component of ensuring the security and reliability of web applications. By following established methodologies, leveraging automated tools, and employing advanced testing techniques, security professionals can identify vulnerabilities, assess risks, and ultimately strengthen the security posture of web applications. Continuous learning and staying informed about evolving threats are key to being effective in this ever-changing field.

Web applications have grown increasingly complex, offering a wide range of features and functionality to users. While these advancements enhance the user experience, they also introduce complexity into the codebase, which can lead to a myriad of security vulnerabilities. Next, we delve into the world of complex web application vulnerabilities, exploring how attackers exploit them and how security professionals can mitigate the risks.

One of the most complex and potentially devastating vulnerabilities in web applications is Remote Code Execution (RCE). This vulnerability allows an attacker to execute arbitrary code on the server, effectively gaining control over the entire application. Attackers often seek RCE to take over servers, exfiltrate data, or pivot to other parts of the network.

Exploiting RCE vulnerabilities typically involves injecting malicious code, such as PHP, Python, or JavaScript, into *the application. Attackers search for vulnerabilities like unvalidated input, deserialization flaws, or insecure server-side includes (SSI) to achieve RCE. Mitigating RCE risks involves input validation, output encoding, and strong access controls.*

Another complex vulnerability is Server-Side Request Forgery (SSRF), where an attacker tricks the server into making unintended HTTP requests to internal or external resources. Attackers use SSRF to access internal systems, exfiltrate data, or perform reconnaissance. Exploiting SSRF often requires crafting malicious URLs that trigger unwanted requests.

Blind SQL Injection is a sophisticated form of SQL injection where an attacker cannot directly observe the results of their SQL queries. Instead, they infer the results based on the application's behavior. Attackers exploit Blind SQL Injection by crafting SQL queries that trigger true or false conditions, allowing them to extract data or infer its existence.

To mitigate Blind SQL Injection and similar vulnerabilities, input validation, parameterized queries, and output encoding are essential. Web application firewalls (WAFs) can also help detect and block malicious SQL injection attempts.

Cross-Site Request Forgery (CSRF) is a complex vulnerability where an attacker tricks a user into performing actions on a different website without their knowledge or consent. Attackers use CSRF to perform actions like changing passwords, transferring funds, or performing other sensitive operations on behalf of a victim.

Exploiting CSRF vulnerabilities requires creating malicious requests that the victim's browser unknowingly submits. CSRF tokens and SameSite attributes in cookies can help mitigate this risk by validating the origin of incoming requests.

File Upload vulnerabilities can be complex, allowing attackers to upload malicious files that can lead to various exploits, such as RCE or defacement. Attackers often manipulate file extensions or evade content-type checks to upload malicious files.

Mitigating File Upload vulnerabilities involves strict content-type and file extension checks, sandboxed file storage, and regular security updates for server-side software.

Insecure Deserialization is a complex vulnerability where attackers manipulate the deserialization process to execute arbitrary code, gain unauthorized access, or cause application logic to behave unexpectedly. Exploiting insecure deserialization often requires crafting malicious payloads within serialized data.

To protect against insecure deserialization, input validation, and the use of safe deserialization libraries are crucial. Additionally, implementing proper access controls and monitoring for anomalous deserialization behavior can help detect and prevent attacks.

Exploiting complex vulnerabilities requires a deep understanding of the application's architecture and potential attack vectors. Attackers often engage in reconnaissance to identify weak points and gather information about the target. Security professionals can counter this by conducting thorough security assessments, including penetration testing and code reviews.

Web application security tools like Burp Suite, OWASP ZAP, and Acunetix can help identify complex vulnerabilities by simulating attacks and analyzing application responses. However, manual testing is often necessary to uncover more subtle vulnerabilities that automated tools may miss.

Regular security training and awareness programs for development teams are essential to ensure that developers are well-informed about complex vulnerabilities and how to mitigate them during the software development lifecycle. Security professionals should work closely with development teams to promote secure coding practices and conduct code reviews.

In summary, complex web application vulnerabilities pose significant risks to the security and integrity of web applications. Attackers continuously evolve their techniques to exploit these vulnerabilities, making it crucial for security professionals to stay vigilant and proactive in identifying and mitigating these threats. By understanding the intricacies of complex vulnerabilities and employing best practices for secure coding and testing, organizations can better defend their web applications against sophisticated attacks.

Chapter 6: Exploiting IoT and Embedded Systems

The Internet of Things (IoT) has ushered in a new era of interconnected devices and systems that promise to revolutionize our daily lives. From smart thermostats and wearable fitness trackers to industrial sensors and autonomous vehicles, IoT devices have become ubiquitous. However, this proliferation of IoT devices also brings a host of security challenges, as these devices often exhibit vulnerabilities that can be exploited by malicious actors. Next, we will explore the vulnerabilities in IoT devices and systems, their implications, and strategies to mitigate these risks.

One of the primary vulnerabilities in IoT devices is the use of default credentials. Manufacturers often ship IoT devices with default usernames and passwords that are rarely changed by end-users. Attackers can easily find lists of default credentials for various devices on the internet and use them to gain unauthorized access.

To address this vulnerability, device manufacturers should enforce password changes upon initial setup, encourage strong, unique passwords, and implement mechanisms to prevent the use of default credentials. Additionally, end-users must be educated about the importance of changing default passwords.

Insecure firmware and software updates present another significant vulnerability in IoT devices. Manufacturers may not prioritize security patches, or users may neglect to install updates. Attackers can exploit unpatched vulnerabilities to compromise devices or gain access to networks.

Device manufacturers should establish a robust system for delivering security updates and patches promptly. Users must be informed about the importance of updating their IoT devices regularly to ensure their security.

Many IoT devices lack proper authentication and authorization mechanisms. Some devices may not require any form of authentication, while others use weak or easily guessable credentials. Attackers can exploit these weaknesses to impersonate authorized users or gain unauthorized access.

Manufacturers should implement strong authentication mechanisms, such as multi-factor authentication, and ensure that users cannot access device features or data without proper authorization. User roles and permissions should be clearly defined and enforced.

Inadequate encryption of data in transit and at rest is a common vulnerability in IoT devices and systems. Attackers can intercept and manipulate data when it is transmitted between the device and the cloud or stored on the device itself.

Manufacturers should prioritize the use of strong encryption protocols for data in transit and at rest. Additionally, they should provide users with options to encrypt sensitive data stored on the device. End-users should be educated on the importance of data encryption and its role in maintaining privacy and security.

IoT devices often lack sufficient protection against physical attacks. Attackers can physically access devices, extract sensitive information, or tamper with device functionality.

Manufacturers should consider physical security measures, such as tamper-evident seals, secure boot processes, and hardware-based encryption, to protect devices from physical attacks. End-users should also be informed about best practices for securing IoT devices physically.

Interoperability and integration of IoT devices with other systems can introduce vulnerabilities. Devices may not properly authenticate or validate the data they receive from other devices or systems, allowing attackers to inject malicious data or manipulate device interactions.

Manufacturers should adhere to established standards and best practices for interoperability and integration. They should implement robust data validation and authentication processes to ensure the integrity and security of device interactions.

IoT devices may have weak or non-existent update mechanisms, making it challenging to apply security patches or update firmware. As a result, devices may remain vulnerable to known exploits.

Manufacturers should design devices with the ability to receive and install updates securely. Regular updates should be part of the device's lifecycle, and manufacturers should provide support for an extended period to ensure the ongoing security of IoT devices.

Inadequate logging and monitoring capabilities are a vulnerability in many IoT devices. Without *comprehensive logging and monitoring, it can be challenging to detect and respond to security incidents or anomalous behavior.*

Manufacturers should implement robust logging and monitoring features in IoT devices, enabling users to track device activities and detect potential security breaches. End-users should be educated on how to review logs and respond to security alerts.

In summary, IoT devices and systems offer tremendous potential but also introduce vulnerabilities that can have far-reaching consequences. Manufacturers, developers, and end-users must work together to address these vulnerabilities and ensure the security and privacy of IoT ecosystems. By implementing best practices for securing IoT devices, staying informed about emerging threats, and prioritizing regular updates and patches, we can harness the benefits of IoT while minimizing the associated risks.

Chapter 7: Cloud Security and Penetration Testing

The adoption of cloud computing has transformed the way organizations manage their IT infrastructure and services. The cloud offers scalability, flexibility, and cost-effectiveness, making it an attractive option for businesses of all sizes. However, this shift to the cloud also brings a new set of security challenges that organizations must address to protect their data and applications. Next, we will explore the cloud security challenges and the solutions available to mitigate these risks.

One of the primary challenges in cloud security is data protection. When data is stored in the cloud, it is no longer within the physical confines of an organization's data center. This introduces concerns about data confidentiality, integrity, and availability. Unauthorized access, data breaches, and data loss are significant concerns.

To address data protection challenges, organizations can implement strong encryption mechanisms for data both in transit and at rest. Encryption ensures that even if data is accessed by unauthorized parties, it remains unintelligible without the proper decryption keys. Additionally, access controls and identity management solutions can help restrict access to sensitive data only to authorized users.

Another critical challenge in cloud security is identity and access management (IAM). With cloud services, users can access resources from anywhere, making it essential to manage identities and access permissions effectively. Unauthorized access or compromised credentials can lead to security breaches.

Organizations should implement robust IAM solutions that include multi-factor authentication, single sign-on, and role-based access controls. By ensuring that only authorized individuals can access cloud resources and enforcing strong authentication, the risk of unauthorized access is minimized.

Compliance and regulatory requirements present a significant challenge for organizations using cloud services. Different regions and industries have specific regulations regarding data privacy and security, such as GDPR in Europe or HIPAA in healthcare. Non-compliance can result in legal consequences and reputational damage.

To address compliance challenges, organizations must choose cloud providers that offer compliance certifications relevant to their industry. Additionally, they should implement monitoring and auditing solutions to track compliance with regulatory requirements and maintain proper documentation.

Cloud providers offer a shared responsibility model, where they are responsible for the security of the cloud infrastructure, while customers are responsible for securing their data and applications within the cloud. This division of responsibility can be a challenge for organizations that may not fully understand their security responsibilities.

To address this challenge, organizations must educate their staff and establish clear policies and procedures for cloud security. Training and awareness programs help ensure that employees understand their roles and responsibilities in securing cloud resources.

The dynamic nature of cloud environments presents challenges in terms of visibility and control. With resources being provisioned and de-provisioned rapidly, organizations may struggle to maintain an accurate inventory of assets and track changes to configurations.

Cloud security solutions can help address this challenge by providing real-time monitoring and alerting capabilities. Automated tools can detect changes to configurations and assess them against security best practices, ensuring that resources remain in a secure state.

A lack of transparency and visibility into cloud provider security practices is a common concern. Organizations may not have full insight into how their cloud provider secures the underlying infrastructure.

To address this challenge, organizations can choose cloud providers that are transparent about their security practices and provide regular updates on security features and enhancements. Additionally, third-party security assessments and audits can provide independent verification of a cloud provider's security posture.

Security incident response in the cloud can be challenging due to the distributed nature of cloud environments. Detecting and responding to incidents across multiple cloud services and regions requires a well-defined incident response plan.

Organizations should develop and regularly test their incident response plans for cloud environments. This includes defining roles and responsibilities, establishing communication channels, and coordinating incident response efforts with the cloud provider.

The use of containers and serverless computing introduces unique security challenges. Containers may share the same underlying host OS, creating potential attack vectors, while serverless functions may execute in shared runtime environments, posing security risks.

To address container security challenges, organizations should implement container orchestration tools with built-in security features and practices such as image scanning and least privilege access. For serverless security, organizations should use security-focused coding practices and rely on the cloud provider's security controls.

Finally, the rapid adoption of DevOps practices and continuous integration/continuous deployment (CI/CD) pipelines can introduce security vulnerabilities if not properly integrated into the development process.

To address this challenge, organizations should implement security as code (SaC) practices, which integrate security checks and testing into the CI/CD pipeline. This ensures that security is a fundamental part of the software development lifecycle.

In summary, cloud security is a critical consideration for organizations leveraging cloud services. While the cloud offers numerous benefits, it also introduces a unique set of challenges that require careful planning and implementation of security measures. By addressing data protection, IAM, compliance, education, visibility, transparency, incident response, container and serverless security, and integrating security into DevOps practices, organizations can enhance their cloud security posture and protect their data and applications in the cloud environment.

As organizations increasingly adopt cloud-based services and infrastructure, the need for comprehensive security assessments becomes paramount. Penetration testing, a crucial component of any security strategy, is equally important in cloud-based environments as it is in traditional on-premises setups. Next, we will delve into the intricacies of conducting penetration testing in cloud-based environments, exploring the unique challenges and methodologies involved.

Before embarking on a penetration test in a cloud-based environment, it is essential to define clear objectives and scope for the engagement. This includes specifying the target systems, services, and cloud providers that will be assessed. The objectives should align with the organization's security goals and compliance requirements.

A critical consideration when conducting penetration testing in the cloud is the choice of the cloud service models: Infrastructure as a Service (IaaS), Platform as a Service (PaaS), or Software as a Service (SaaS). Each model offers a different level of control and responsibility, affecting the scope and methodologies of the test.

In an IaaS environment, the organization has more control over the infrastructure, making it essential to assess the security configuration of virtual machines, network settings, and access controls. PaaS environments focus on application development, requiring a thorough evaluation of the application layer, while SaaS environments require assessments of the application's security and data protection.

In the cloud, it is crucial to understand the shared responsibility model, which delineates the security responsibilities between the cloud provider and the customer. While the cloud provider is responsible for securing the underlying infrastructure, customers are accountable for securing their data and applications within the cloud. This understanding guides the penetration tester in identifying potential vulnerabilities and misconfigurations.

One of the fundamental aspects of penetration testing in the cloud is the assessment of identity and access management (IAM). Proper IAM practices are critical for controlling access to cloud resources. Penetration testers should examine the effectiveness of IAM policies, roles, and permissions, looking for vulnerabilities that could lead to unauthorized access.

To conduct IAM assessments, penetration testers may attempt to exploit weak access controls, perform privilege escalation attacks, or assess the effectiveness of multi-factor authentication (MFA). Verifying that users have only the permissions they need is essential to reduce the attack surface.

Another significant aspect of cloud penetration testing is the evaluation of network security controls. In a cloud environment, virtual networks, firewalls, and security groups play a crucial role in protecting assets. Penetration testers must assess the security posture of these network components, checking for misconfigurations and vulnerabilities.

Common assessments include testing for exposed ports, analyzing network segmentation, and identifying weaknesses in firewall rules. The objective is to ensure that network security measures effectively safeguard cloud resources from unauthorized access.

The cloud's dynamic nature, characterized by the rapid provisioning and de-provisioning of resources, presents challenges for vulnerability management. Traditional penetration testing may not be sufficient to address this dynamic environment. Therefore, continuous security monitoring and automation become critical.

To adapt to the cloud's dynamic nature, penetration testers can employ automation tools to detect changes in configurations, assess new assets, and identify vulnerabilities in real-time. Automation enhances the ability to keep up with the evolving cloud environment and maintain security.

While penetration testing in the cloud shares similarities with traditional testing, it also introduces new considerations. For example, cloud-based applications and services may rely on serverless computing, which involves executing code without managing the underlying infrastructure. Penetration testers must understand how serverless functions work and identify security vulnerabilities specific to this technology.

Moreover, cloud environments often leverage containerization technologies like Docker and Kubernetes. Penetration testers should have expertise in assessing container security, including analyzing container images for vulnerabilities and evaluating container orchestration platforms for misconfigurations.

When conducting penetration tests in the cloud, it is vital to prioritize data security. Data breaches can have severe consequences, and ensuring the confidentiality and integrity of data is paramount. Penetration testers should focus on assessing data encryption practices, data storage configurations, and access controls related to sensitive data.

A key consideration is the compliance landscape in which the organization operates. Many industries have specific compliance requirements that must be met. Penetration testers should align their assessments with these compliance standards, ensuring that the cloud environment adheres to regulatory requirements.

Throughout the penetration testing engagement, clear communication with both the organization's internal teams and the cloud provider is essential. Collaboration helps address issues promptly and ensures that all parties are aware of the testing activities, minimizing disruptions to cloud services.

In summary, penetration testing in cloud-based environments is a vital component of ensuring the security of cloud infrastructure and applications. It requires a thorough understanding of the shared responsibility model, the specific cloud service model, IAM practices, network security controls, automation, serverless and container technologies, data security, compliance, and effective communication. By addressing these considerations, organizations can identify and remediate vulnerabilities in their cloud environments, enhancing overall security.

Chapter 8: Red Teaming and Scenario-Based Testing

Red teaming is a proactive approach to testing an organization's security by simulating real-world attacks. Next, we will explore red team operations and methodologies, providing insights into the techniques and strategies used by red teams to assess an organization's defenses.

The primary objective of a red team is to identify vulnerabilities and weaknesses in an organization's security posture. Red team exercises are designed to mimic the tactics, techniques, and procedures (TTPs) employed by malicious actors, allowing organizations to understand their susceptibility to various cyber threats.

Before diving into the methodologies used by red teams, it is essential to establish the goals and scope of a red team engagement. Organizations must define the specific objectives they want to achieve through the exercise. This could range from assessing the effectiveness of their incident response procedures to identifying vulnerabilities in critical systems.

Once the goals are defined, the red team begins by conducting reconnaissance. Reconnaissance involves gathering information about the target organization, including its infrastructure, employees, technologies, and security controls. This phase helps the red team understand the organization's attack surface and potential entry points.

Red teamers employ various techniques during the reconnaissance phase, such as open-source intelligence

(OSINT) gathering, social engineering, and network scanning. They aim to collect as much information as possible to inform their attack strategy.

With reconnaissance completed, the red team moves on to the planning phase. In this phase, they formulate attack scenarios and strategies based on the information gathered. The red team plans how they will attempt to breach the organization's defenses, identifying potential vulnerabilities and attack vectors.

A critical aspect of red team planning is the development of attack profiles. These profiles outline the personas and techniques the red team will use to simulate different threat actors. By creating these profiles, the red team can emulate various cyber adversaries, such as nation-state hackers, hacktivists, or insider threats.

Once the attack scenarios are defined, the red team begins the execution phase. This is where they put their attack plans into action, attempting to breach the organization's defenses using the selected attack vectors. Red teamers use a combination of technical skills and social engineering tactics to simulate real-world attacks.

During the execution phase, red teamers may attempt to exploit vulnerabilities, gain unauthorized access to systems, escalate privileges, and move laterally within the organization's network. Their goal is to identify weaknesses that could be exploited by malicious actors.

As the red team progresses through the engagement, they may encounter defensive measures put in place by the organization, such as intrusion detection systems

(IDS), intrusion prevention systems (IPS), and security information and event management (SIEM) solutions. Red teamers must adapt their tactics to evade detection and maintain stealth.

One of the key principles of red teaming is to provide realistic feedback to the organization. As such, red teams aim to document their actions, findings, and methodologies thoroughly. This documentation allows the organization to understand the attack techniques employed and the vulnerabilities exposed during the engagement.

After the execution phase is completed, the red team conducts a debriefing with the organization's stakeholders. During this debriefing, the red team shares their findings, discusses the impact of successful attacks, and provides recommendations for improving security. The goal is to help the organization enhance its security posture based on the lessons learned from the red team exercise.

In addition to traditional red team operations, organizations may also engage in purple teaming. Purple teaming is a collaborative approach that involves both the red team (attackers) and the blue team (defenders). The two teams work together to assess and improve security by sharing information, testing defenses, and validating security controls.

Purple teaming allows organizations to better understand how their security measures perform under simulated attacks. It fosters cooperation between offensive and defensive teams, leading to more effective security practices.

To maintain the effectiveness of red team operations, it is essential to conduct periodic assessments. Regular red team engagements help organizations stay vigilant and adapt to evolving threats. Red teams can test newly implemented security measures and ensure that existing vulnerabilities have been addressed.

In summary, red team operations and methodologies are valuable tools for organizations seeking to assess and improve their security posture. By simulating real-world attacks and employing a combination of technical skills and social engineering tactics, red teams help organizations identify vulnerabilities and weaknesses in their defenses. The insights gained from red team engagements enable organizations to enhance their security measures, ultimately better protecting their assets and data.

Scenario-based testing and simulation play a crucial role in evaluating an organization's cybersecurity preparedness. These approaches involve creating real-world scenarios that mimic potential cyber threats and attacks to assess an organization's ability to respond effectively.

The value of scenario-based testing lies in its ability to provide a realistic assessment of an organization's cybersecurity posture. By simulating specific scenarios, organizations can gauge their readiness and identify areas for improvement in incident response, threat detection, and mitigation strategies.

To conduct scenario-based testing effectively, organizations must first define their objectives. They should determine what specific threats or scenarios they want to simulate, such as a ransomware attack, a data breach, or a distributed denial-of-service (DDoS) attack. These objectives will guide the creation of the scenarios.

Once the objectives are established, organizations should design detailed scenarios that replicate the tactics, techniques, and procedures (TTPs) of potential threat actors. This involves crafting a narrative that outlines the scenario's context, the motivations of the attackers, and the steps they would take to achieve their goals.

The scenarios should also specify the attack vectors that will be used, such as phishing emails, malware infections, or social engineering tactics. Additionally, organizations should define the scope of the scenarios, including the systems, networks, and personnel that will be involved.

A critical aspect of scenario-based testing is the involvement of various stakeholders within the organization. This includes IT teams, security personnel, incident responders, and even executives. The goal is to assess how well different teams collaborate and communicate during a cyber incident.

During the testing phase, organizations should execute the scenarios as realistically as possible. This may involve sending simulated phishing emails to employees, deploying malware in controlled environments, or launching simulated attacks against network infrastructure.

The responses of personnel and systems to these scenarios are closely monitored and evaluated. This includes assessing how quickly and effectively the *organization detects the simulated threats, how it responds to incidents, and how it mitigates the potential impact.*

Scenario-based testing also allows organizations to evaluate the effectiveness of their incident response plans and playbooks. It provides an opportunity to identify gaps in these plans and make necessary adjustments to improve them.

One important aspect of scenario-based testing is the collection of data and metrics. Organizations should document the key performance indicators (KPIs) associated with each scenario, such as the time taken to detect an incident, the time taken to respond, and the effectiveness of mitigation measures.

The data collected during scenario-based testing can be used to create post-exercise reports and analysis. These reports provide insights into the organization's strengths and weaknesses in handling cyber threats and incidents.

In addition to evaluating incident response capabilities, scenario-based testing can also assess the effectiveness of security controls and technologies. Organizations can determine if their antivirus software, intrusion detection systems, and firewalls are capable of detecting and mitigating simulated threats.

To maximize the benefits of scenario-based testing, organizations should conduct these exercises regularly. Cyber threats evolve constantly, and new attack techniques emerge regularly. Regular testing ensures that an organization's defenses remain robust and adaptable to changing threat landscapes.

Scenario-based testing can also be used to test the resilience of critical infrastructure and services. Organizations can simulate attacks on specific systems or networks to assess their ability to maintain operations during cyber incidents.

Furthermore, organizations can use scenario-based testing to train their personnel. By exposing employees to realistic cyber threats and incidents, organizations can improve their staff's readiness to handle real-world situations.

In summary, scenario-based testing and simulation are valuable tools for assessing an organization's cybersecurity preparedness. By creating and executing realistic scenarios, organizations can evaluate their incident response capabilities, identify areas for improvement, and enhance their overall cybersecurity posture. Regular testing ensures that organizations remain resilient in the face of evolving cyber threats and helps them protect their assets and data effectively.

Chapter 9: Incident Response and Digital Forensics

Incident response is a critical component of cybersecurity, and organizations must establish effective best practices to minimize the impact of security incidents and data breaches. Next, we will explore incident response best practices that help organizations detect, manage, and recover from cyber incidents.

Establish an Incident Response Plan: The foundation of incident response is a well-defined and documented plan that outlines the steps to take when a security incident occurs. This plan should be comprehensive and cover various types of incidents, from malware infections to data breaches.

Designate an Incident Response Team: Create a dedicated incident response team comprising individuals with the necessary skills and expertise. This team should include IT personnel, cybersecurity experts, legal counsel, and communication professionals.

Define Incident Categories: Categorize incidents based on their severity and potential impact on the organization. This helps in prioritizing responses and resource allocation.

Implement an Incident Detection System: Deploy monitoring and detection tools to identify unusual or suspicious activities on the network. This includes intrusion detection systems (IDS), intrusion prevention systems (IPS), and security information and event management (SIEM) solutions.

Continuous Monitoring: Monitor network and system logs in real-time to detect anomalies or signs of a security breach. Timely detection can significantly reduce the impact of an incident.

Incident Classification: When an incident occurs, classify it based on its severity and impact. This classification will determine the level of response and resources required.

Containment: Act swiftly to contain the incident, isolating affected systems or networks to prevent further damage or data loss. This may involve disabling compromised accounts, blocking malicious traffic, or quarantining infected devices.

Preserve Evidence: Preserve digital evidence related to the incident, as this may be crucial for legal or investigative purposes. Ensure that evidence is collected and stored following proper forensic procedures.

Notification and Communication: Establish clear communication channels within the incident response team and with relevant stakeholders, such as senior management, legal counsel, and law enforcement if necessary.

Legal and Regulatory Compliance: Be aware of legal and regulatory requirements related to incident reporting and data breaches. Comply with these requirements, as failure to do so may lead to legal consequences.

Documentation: Maintain thorough records of the incident, including all actions taken, communications, and decisions made during the response process. This documentation is essential for post-incident analysis and reporting.

Root Cause Analysis: After containing the incident, conduct a detailed analysis to determine the root cause and identify vulnerabilities or weaknesses in the organization's security posture.

Remediation and Recovery: Develop a plan for remediating the vulnerabilities that led to the incident and for restoring affected systems to normal operation. This may involve patching software, updating configurations, or enhancing security controls.

Testing and Validation: Verify that the remediation efforts are effective and that systems are secure before returning them to the production environment. Testing is crucial to ensure that similar incidents do not recur.

Post-Incident Review: Conduct a post-incident review with the incident response team to assess the effectiveness of the response and identify areas for improvement. Use these lessons learned to update and enhance the incident response plan.

Training and Awareness: Regularly train employees and raise awareness about incident response procedures and best practices. All personnel should know how to recognize and report security incidents.

Tabletop Exercises: Conduct tabletop exercises and simulations to test the incident response plan and the team's readiness. These exercises help identify gaps and areas that need improvement.

Continuous Improvement: Incident response is an ongoing process. Continuously update the incident response plan based on emerging threats, changes in the organization's infrastructure, and lessons learned from previous incidents.

External Support: Establish relationships with external incident response teams, law enforcement agencies, and cybersecurity experts who can provide assistance and expertise during major incidents.

Public Relations Strategy: Develop a public relations and communication strategy for handling incidents that may impact the organization's reputation. Transparency and timely communication are essential.

Post-Incident Analysis: After an incident is resolved, conduct a comprehensive analysis to understand the full scope of the impact, assess the effectiveness of the response, and identify areas for further improvement.

Cyber Insurance: Consider obtaining cyber insurance to mitigate financial losses associated with security incidents and data breaches.

Data Backup and Recovery: Regularly back up critical data and systems to ensure data integrity and availability in the event of an incident.

Incident Response Playbooks: Develop specific incident response playbooks for different types of incidents to streamline the response process and ensure consistency.

External Collaboration: Collaborate with industry peers and information sharing organizations to stay informed about emerging threats and to share insights and best practices.

Executive Involvement: Ensure that senior management is actively involved in incident response efforts and understands the importance of cybersecurity.

Continuous Monitoring and Threat Intelligence: Implement continuous threat monitoring and leverage threat intelligence feeds to stay ahead of evolving threats and vulnerabilities.

In summary, incident response is a critical aspect of cybersecurity that requires a well-structured plan and a proactive approach. By following these best practices, organizations can effectively detect, respond to, and recover from security incidents, minimizing their impact and reducing the risk of future incidents.

Digital forensics is the process of collecting, preserving, analyzing, and presenting electronic evidence in a way that is admissible in a court of law. It plays a crucial role in investigating cybercrimes, data breaches, and other digital incidents. Next, we will delve into various digital forensics tools and techniques used by professionals in this field.

Forensic Imaging: One of the fundamental steps in digital forensics is creating a forensic image of the digital evidence. This process involves making an exact copy of the storage media, ensuring that no alterations or changes are made to the original data.

Forensic Imaging Software: To create forensic images, professionals use specialized software like AccessData FTK Imager, EnCase, and dd (a command-line tool in Unix-like operating systems).

Chain of Custody: Maintaining a chain of custody is crucial to preserving the integrity of digital evidence. It documents the handling of evidence from the moment it is collected to its presentation in court.

Write-Blocking: Write-blocking devices and software are used to prevent any write operations to the evidence storage media during the imaging process, ensuring that the original data remains unchanged.

Volatility Analysis: Volatility is a framework for analyzing the volatile memory (RAM) of a computer. It helps in identifying running processes, open network connections, and other valuable information during a live system analysis.

File Carving: File carving tools, such as Scalpel and PhotoRec, are used to recover deleted or fragmented files from storage media by identifying file signatures and reconstructing them.

Keyword Searching: Digital forensics professionals use keyword searching to identify relevant files or data within a large dataset. Tools like Autopsy and X-Ways Forensics provide keyword search capabilities.

Metadata Analysis: Metadata contains information about files, such as creation dates, modification dates, and authorship. Examining metadata can be crucial in investigations. Metadata analysis tools help in extracting and analyzing this information.

File Hashing: Hashing algorithms like MD5, SHA-1, and SHA-256 are used to generate hash values for files. These hashes can be compared to verify the integrity of files or to identify known malicious files.

Timeline Analysis: Creating a timeline of events based on file timestamps and system logs can provide valuable insights into the sequence of activities on a system. Timeline analysis tools like Plaso and log2timeline help in constructing timelines.

Registry Analysis: Windows Registry is a critical source of information for digital forensics. Tools like Registry

Explorer and RegRipper assist in analyzing the Windows Registry for evidence.

Email Forensics: Email is often a significant source of evidence in investigations. Email forensic tools like MailXaminer and Emailchemy help in analyzing email messages, attachments, and email headers.

Mobile Device Forensics: Mobile devices store a wealth of data. Tools like Cellebrite and Oxygen Forensic Detective are used to extract data from smartphones and tablets, including call logs, messages, and app data.

Network Forensics: Network forensics involves monitoring and analyzing network traffic to identify security incidents and trace malicious activities. Tools like Wireshark and NetworkMiner are commonly used in this area.

Steganography Detection: Steganography is the practice of hiding data within other files or media. Steganalysis tools are used to detect and extract hidden information.

Memory Forensics: Analyzing the contents of a system's RAM can uncover valuable information about running processes, network connections, and malware. Tools like Volatility and Rekall are used for memory forensics.

File Recovery: When files are deleted or lost, file recovery tools like Recuva and TestDisk can help in retrieving them from storage media.

Forensic Reporting: After completing the analysis, digital forensics professionals prepare detailed reports that document their findings, the techniques used, and the evidence collected. These reports must be clear, concise, and admissible in court.

Legal Considerations: Digital forensics professionals must adhere to legal and ethical standards when collecting and analyzing evidence. They should be aware of relevant laws and regulations, chain of custody requirements, and rules of evidence.

Expert Testimony: In many cases, digital forensics experts are called to testify in court about their findings. They must be able to explain their processes, methodologies, and conclusions to judges and juries.

Continuing Education: Digital forensics is an evolving field, and professionals must stay up-to-date with the latest tools, techniques, and trends. Continuous learning and training are essential.

Quality Assurance: Quality assurance practices, such as validation and verification of tools and methodologies, are crucial to ensuring the accuracy and reliability of digital forensics investigations.

Digital forensics is a multidisciplinary field that requires a combination of technical skills, legal knowledge, and attention to detail. The tools and techniques discussed Next are essential for conducting effective and thorough digital investigations.

Chapter 10: Ethical Hacking Certifications and Career Development

Selecting the appropriate certification path is a critical decision for anyone aspiring to enter the field of ethical hacking and cybersecurity. The right certification can open doors to exciting career opportunities, validate your skills and knowledge, and increase your earning potential. However, with numerous certification options available, it can be challenging to determine which one aligns best with your career goals and interests.

To make an informed decision, it's essential to understand the various certification programs, their focus areas, and their industry recognition. The following sections will guide you through the process of choosing the right certification path for your ethical hacking journey.

Assess Your Goals: Start by defining your career objectives and aspirations. Are you interested in becoming a penetration tester, a security analyst, a network defender, or a digital forensics expert? Your chosen career path will influence the certifications you should pursue.

Entry-Level Certifications: If you are new to the field, consider starting with entry-level certifications such as CompTIA Security+ or Certified Information Systems Security Professional (CISSP) to build a solid foundation in cybersecurity.

Penetration Testing: If your goal is to become a penetration tester, certifications like Certified Ethical

Hacker (CEH), Offensive Security Certified Professional (OSCP), or CompTIA PenTest+ are highly regarded and focus on offensive security techniques.

Network Security: For those interested in network security, certifications like Certified Information Systems Security Professional (CISSP), Certified Information Security Manager (CISM), and Certified Information Systems Auditor (CISA) are valuable.

Security Analyst: Aspiring security analysts should consider certifications such as Certified Information Systems Security Professional (CISSP), CompTIA Security+, Certified Information Security Manager (CISM), and Certified Information Systems Auditor (CISA).

Digital Forensics: If you want to specialize in digital forensics, certifications like Certified Computer Examiner (CCE), Certified Forensic Computer Examiner (CFCE), and GIAC Certified Forensic Analyst (GCFA) are highly relevant.

Cloud Security: As cloud computing continues to grow, certifications like Certified Cloud Security Professional (CCSP) and AWS Certified Security - Specialty are essential for professionals working with cloud-based systems.

Vendor-Specific Certifications: Many technology companies offer certifications specific to their products and platforms. Examples include Cisco Certified Network Associate (CCNA) for networking and Certified Information Systems Security Professional (CISSP) for information security.

Consult with Professionals: Reach out to experienced professionals in the field or mentors who have already achieved the certifications you're interested in. They can provide valuable insights and guidance based on their experiences.

Research Industry Demand: Investigate the demand for specific certifications in your desired job market or industry. Some certifications may be more valuable in certain regions or sectors.

Cost and Resources: Consider the cost and resources required for each certification, including training materials, exam fees, and study time. Ensure that the certification aligns with your budget and available resources.

Time Commitment: Assess the time required to prepare for each certification exam. Some certifications may demand more extensive study and hands-on experience.

Practice Labs and Hands-On Experience: Practical skills are essential in cybersecurity. Look for certifications that offer hands-on labs and real-world scenarios to apply your knowledge.

Exam Difficulty: Evaluate the difficulty level of each certification exam. Some certifications have reputations for being particularly challenging, while others are more accessible for beginners.

Continuing Education: Determine whether the certification requires ongoing maintenance through continuing education or renewal exams. It's crucial to factor in long-term commitments.

Networking Opportunities: Some certifications provide access to exclusive professional networks and communities, which can be beneficial for career growth and knowledge sharing.

Customize Your Path: Don't feel limited by a single certification track. It's common for professionals to pursue multiple certifications to diversify their skills and knowledge.

Choosing the right certification path is a significant step in your journey towards a successful career in ethical hacking and cybersecurity. Take the time to research, consult with experts, and align your choices with your career goals. Remember that certifications are just one part of your cybersecurity skillset, and practical experience remains invaluable in this dynamic field.

The field of ethical hacking and cybersecurity is dynamic and ever-evolving, offering numerous opportunities for career advancement and personal growth. Whether you're just starting or looking to take your existing career to the next level, there are various strategies and considerations to help you advance in this exciting and challenging industry.

Continuous Learning: The first and most crucial step in advancing your career in ethical hacking and cybersecurity is a commitment to continuous learning. Technology and cyber threats evolve rapidly, and staying up-to-date with the latest trends, tools, and techniques is essential.

Networking: Building a strong professional network is vital in this field. Attend industry conferences, join online forums and communities, and connect with colleagues in the cybersecurity industry. Networking can open doors to job opportunities and provide valuable insights.

Certifications: Consider pursuing advanced certifications that align with your career goals. Certifications such as Certified Information Systems Security Professional (CISSP), Certified Information Security Manager (CISM), and Certified Information Systems Auditor (CISA) are highly regarded and can enhance your credibility.

Specialization: Identify a niche or specialization within cybersecurity that interests you the most. Specializations can include penetration testing, incident response, digital forensics, cloud security, and more. Focusing on a specific area can make you an expert in that field.

Hands-On Experience: Practical experience is invaluable. Seek opportunities to work on real-world projects, either through internships, part-time positions, or volunteer work. Hands-on experience helps you apply theoretical knowledge and develop practical skills.

Advanced Training: Invest in advanced training courses and workshops. Many organizations offer specialized training programs for cybersecurity professionals. These programs can provide in-depth knowledge and hands-on experience in specific areas.

Stay Informed: Regularly read cybersecurity news, research papers, and blogs to stay informed about emerging threats and trends. Being aware of the latest developments in the field can help you adapt and respond effectively.

Contribute to Open Source Projects: Contributing to open-source security projects not only allows you to give back to the community but also helps you gain practical experience and collaborate with experts in the field.

Soft Skills: Develop soft skills such as communication, teamwork, and problem-solving. Effective communication is crucial when explaining complex security concepts or incidents to non-technical stakeholders.

Ethical Hacking Labs: Set up your ethical hacking lab environment to practice and refine your skills safely. Experiment with different tools and techniques, and document your findings and experiments.

Mentorship: Seek out mentors in the cybersecurity industry who can provide guidance and mentorship. Experienced professionals can offer valuable insights and help you navigate your career path.

Public Speaking and Writing: Consider sharing your knowledge through public speaking engagements or writing articles and blogs. Speaking at conferences or publishing research can establish you as an authority in the field.

Soft Skills: Develop soft skills such as communication, teamwork, and problem-solving. Effective communication is crucial when explaining complex security concepts or incidents to non-technical stakeholders.

Ethical Hacking Labs: Set up your ethical hacking lab environment to practice and refine your skills safely. Experiment with different tools and techniques, and document your findings and experiments.

Mentorship: Seek out mentors in the cybersecurity industry who can provide guidance and mentorship. Experienced professionals can offer valuable insights and help you navigate your career path.

Public Speaking and Writing: Consider sharing your knowledge through public speaking engagements or writing articles and blogs. Speaking at conferences or publishing research can establish you as an authority in the field.

Cybersecurity Policies and Governance: Understand the importance of cybersecurity policies and governance within organizations. Knowledge of regulatory frameworks and compliance is increasingly valuable.

Management and Leadership: If you aspire to leadership roles, consider pursuing management or leadership training. Cybersecurity managers need a combination of technical expertise and leadership skills.

Cybersecurity Ethics: Always prioritize ethics in your work. Ethical hacking is about improving security, not causing harm. Adhere to a strong ethical code and respect legal boundaries.

Professional Associations: Join professional associations such as (ISC)², ISACA, or CompTIA's IT Security Community. These organizations offer resources, networking opportunities, and industry recognition.

Adaptability: Be adaptable and ready to pivot as the cybersecurity landscape changes. New technologies, threats, and challenges will continue to emerge, so flexibility is key to long-term success.

Cybersecurity Culture: Promote a cybersecurity culture within organizations. Educate colleagues and employees about security best practices and the importance of cybersecurity.

Job Search and Interviews: When seeking new job opportunities, tailor your resume and interview responses to highlight your relevant skills and experiences. Be prepared to demonstrate your technical knowledge.

Continuous Improvement: Finally, never stop striving for improvement. The field of ethical hacking and cybersecurity is a lifelong learning journey, and there is always more to discover and explore.

In summary, advancing your career in ethical hacking and cybersecurity requires dedication, continuous learning, practical experience, and a commitment to ethical conduct. By following these strategies and staying proactive in your professional development, you can achieve your career goals and contribute to the ever-important mission of protecting digital assets and information.

Conclusion

In this comprehensive book bundle, "PENTESTING 101: CRACKING GADGETS AND HACKING SOFTWARE," we embarked on a journey through the exciting world of ethical hacking and cybersecurity. Through four distinct volumes, we explored the key aspects of penetration testing, network security, web application security, and advanced cybersecurity techniques.

"BOOK 1 - PENTESTING 101: A BEGINNER'S GUIDE TO ETHICAL HACKING" served as our foundation, introducing us to the fundamental concepts and principles of ethical hacking. We learned how to set up our hacking environment, understand the hacker mindset, and employ scanning and enumeration techniques to uncover vulnerabilities.

"BOOK 2 - PENTESTING 101: EXPLOITING VULNERABILITIES IN NETWORK SECURITY" delved deeper into the realm of network security. We discovered the intricacies of exploiting weaknesses in network protocols, gaining unauthorized access to network resources, and intercepting network traffic safely. We also explored the importance of intrusion detection and prevention systems in safeguarding networks.

"BOOK 3 - PENTESTING 101: ADVANCED TECHNIQUES FOR WEB APPLICATION SECURITY" turned our attention to the world of web application security. We learned about the landscape of web application security, delved into authentication and session management testing, and uncovered advanced vulnerabilities. We also explored the critical role of web application firewalls and API security.

"BOOK 4 - PENTESTING 101: MASTERING CYBERSECURITY CHALLENGES AND BEYOND" elevated our skills to new heights,

equipping us with advanced network penetration testing techniques, IoT and embedded systems exploitation, cloud security insights, and real-world ethical hacking scenarios. We also explored incident response, digital forensics, and career development in the field.

Throughout this bundle, we emphasized the importance of ethical hacking as a force for good, aimed at identifying vulnerabilities and enhancing cybersecurity. We embraced the need for continuous learning and adaptability in a field that evolves relentlessly.

As we conclude this journey, remember that the knowledge gained in these pages is not the end but the beginning. Ethical hacking and cybersecurity are ever-changing domains, and staying at the forefront of innovation and security is an ongoing commitment. Whether you're a beginner embarking on your ethical hacking journey or an experienced professional seeking to expand your expertise, the principles and techniques presented in these books will serve as a solid foundation.

We encourage you to apply this knowledge responsibly, with the highest ethical standards, and to contribute positively to the cybersecurity community. With the skills and insights gained from "PENTESTING 101: CRACKING GADGETS AND HACKING SOFTWARE," you are well-equipped to face the challenges and opportunities that the world of ethical hacking and cybersecurity presents. Keep exploring, keep learning, and keep securing the digital landscape. The future of cybersecurity is in your capable hands.